NATIONAL TREATMENT
FOR FOREIGN-CONTROLLED
ENTERPRISES

ORGANISATION FOR ECONOMIC CO-OPERATION AND DEVELOPMENT

Pursuant to article 1 of the Convention signed in Paris on 14th December, 1960, and which came into force on 30th September, 1961, the Organisation for Economic Co-operation and Development (OECD) shall promote policies designed:

- to achieve the highest sustainable economic growth and employment and a rising standard of living in Member countries, while maintaining financial stability, and thus to contribute to the development of the world economy;
- to contribute to sound economic expansion in Member as well as non-member countries in the process of economic development; and
- to contribute to the expansion of world trade on a multilateral, non-discriminatory basis in accordance with international obligations.

The Signatories of the Convention on the OECD are Austria, Belgium, Canada, Denmark, France, the Federal Republic of Germany, Greece, Iceland, Ireland, Italy, Luxembourg, the Netherlands, Norway, Portugal, Spain, Sweden, Switzerland, Turkey, the United Kingdom and the United States. The following countries acceded subsequently to this Convention (the dates are those on which the instruments of accession were deposited): Japan (28th April, 1964), Finland (28th January, 1969), Australia (7th June, 1971) and New Zealand (29th May, 1973).

The Socialist Federal Republic of Yugoslavia takes part in certain work of the OECD (agreement of 28th October, 1961).

Publié en français sous le titre:

**TRAITEMENT NATIONAL DES ENTREPRISES
SOUS CONTRÔLE ÉTRANGER**

In 1976, OECD Member countries declared that enterprises operating in their territory and controlled by nationals of another Member country should be treated not less favourably than domestic enterprises in like situations, that is, should be accorded National Treatment. The OECD's Committee on International Investment and Multinational Enterprises is charged, inter alia, with reviewing the application of National Treatment with a view to extending its application. It is the Committee's view that the application of National Treatment is of considerable importance to the environment for international investment.

A major part of the Committee's efforts in this area has been devoted to clarifying the scope and coverage of the National Treatment instrument and, since 1976, the Committee has issued a number of clarifications with this purpose in mind. On the basis of these, and with the objective of developing a comprehensive view of government measures and policies related to National Treatment, that is, to improving transparency, the Committee has carried out a new and extensive survey of such measures, which has permitted an improved understanding of the measures in effect, of their motivations, and of their relative importance to international investors.

Following the completion of this phase of work on National Treatment, the Committee agreed to recommend publication of this report, which brings together the relevant information concerning this instrument and including its application procedures, clarifications of the instrument and the survey of Member country measures related to National Treatment. The report was de-restricted by the OECD Council on 31st July 1984.

Also available

INTERNATIONAL INVESTMENT AND MULTINATIONAL ENTERPRISES –
REVISED EDITION 1984. Declaration by the Governments of OECD Member Countries
and Decisions of the OECD Council (September 1984)
(21 84 04 1) ISBN 92-64-12603-1   34 pages   £1.80   US$3.50   F18.00

INTERNATIONAL INVESTMENT AND MULTINATIONAL ENTERPRISES –
THE 1984 REVIEW OF THE 1976 DECLARATION AND DECISIONS (July 1984)
(21 84 02 1) ISBN 92-64-12585-X   66 pages   £3.20   US$6.50   F32.00

DISCLOSURE OF INFORMATION BY MULTINATIONAL ENTERPRISES –
CLARIFICATION OF THE ACCOUNTING TERMS IN THE OECD GUIDELINES
(May 1983)
(21 83 02 1) ISBN 92-64-12439-X   48 pages   £3.80   US$7.50   F38.00

INTERNATIONAL INVESTMENT AND MULTINATIONAL ENTERPRISES –
INVESTMENT INCENTIVES AND DISINCENTIVES AND THE INTERNA-
TIONAL INVESTMENT PROCESS (March 1983)
(21 83 01 1) ISBN 92-64-12400-4   250 pages   £8.60   US$17.00   F86.00

INTERNATIONAL INVESTMENT AND MULTINATIONAL ENTERPRISES –
RECENT INTERNATIONAL DIRECT INVESTMENT TRENDS (October 1981)
(21 81 03 1) ISBN 92-64-12250-8   112 pages   £4.60   US$10.00   F46.00

INTERNATIONAL INVESTMENT AND MULTINATIONAL ENTERPRISES –
ACCOUNTING PRACTICES IN OECD MEMBER COUNTRIES (October 1980)
(21 80 05 1) ISBN 92-64-12076-9   250 pages   £6.00   US$13.50   F54.00

CONTROLS AND IMPEDIMENTS AFFECTING INWARD DIRECT INVESTMENT
IN OECD MEMBER COUNTRIES (July 1982)
(21 82 06 1) ISBN 92-64-12344-X   36 pages   £3.00   US$6.00   F30.00

CODE OF LIBERALISATION OF CAPITAL MOVEMENTS – MARCH 1982
EDITION (April 1982)
(21 82 04 1) ISBN 92-64-12070-X   106 pages   £4.90   US$11.00   F49.00

Prices charged at the OECD Publications Office.

*THE OECD CATALOGUE OF PUBLICATIONS and supplements will be sent free of charge
on request addressed either to OECD Publications Office,
2, rue André-Pascal, 75775 PARIS CEDEX 16, or to the OECD Sales Agent in your country.*

TABLE OF CONTENTS

Introduction 7

Chapter I
    The texts of OECD's National Treatment instrument 9

Chapter II
    Implementation procedures for the National Treatment instrument 12

Chapter III
    Clarifications concerning general aspects of the instrument 15

Chapter IV
    Clarifications concerning particular categories of measures 20

Chapter V
    Survey of Member country measures related to National Treatment 35

Notes and References 54

ANNEXES

I.   Member country measures related to National Treatment 57

II.   The OECD Declaration on International Investment and
     Multinational Enterprises, and the Second Revised Decisions
     of the Council on the Guidelines for Multinational Enterprises,
     and on International Investment Incentives and Disincentives ... 143

INTRODUCTION

This publication was prepared to inform the general reader about OECD's National Treatment instrument and its application in Member countries. At the June 1976 meeting of the OECD Council at Ministerial Level, the OECD Member countries adopted the Declaration on International Investment and Multinational Enterprises and several related Decisions, which contain the National Treatment instrument, together with the Guidelines for Multinational Enterprises and the International Investment Incentives and Disincentives instrument (1). The Declaration and Decisions, which have proved to be an important step to extend co-operation among Member countries in the area of international investment and multinational enterprises, were aimed at improving the international investment climate through joint undertakings which strengthen confidence between foreign investors and States (2).

The first paragraph of the National Treatment instrument defines the OECD concept of National Treatment. It states that "Member countries should, consistent with their needs to maintain public order, to protect their essential security interests and to fulfil commitments relating to international peace and security, accord to enterprises operating in their territories and owned or controlled directly or indirectly by nationals of another Member country (hereinafter referred to as "Foreign-Controlled Enterprises") treatment under their laws, regulations and administrative practices, consistent with international law and no less favourable than that accorded in like situations to domestic enterprises (hereinafter referred to as 'National Treatment')." (3) This principle is considered to be central to establishing a favourable climate for foreign investment and to encouraging foreign-controlled enterprises to contribute to economic and social progress. The relevant section of the Declaration also includes provisions indicating that OECD Member countries "will consider applying 'National Treatment' in respect of countries other than Member countries," and "... will endeavour to ensure that their territorial subdivisions apply 'National Treatment'." It is also stated that the Declaration "does not deal with the right of Member countries to regulate the entry of foreign investment or the conditions of esablishment of foreign enterprises." The related Council Decision on National Treatment provides for notification to the OECD of measures taken by a Member country constituting exceptions to National Treatment and for consultations at the request of a Member country in respect of any matter related to this instrument. The complete text of the relevant part of the Declaration and the Decision is given in chapter I of this report.

Responsibility for implementing the application of the National Treatment instrument and reviewing its application is vested in OECD's Committee on International Investment and Multinational Enterprises (hereinafter referred to as "the Committee"), which is composed of representatives of Member country governments. In 1978 the Committee, with the objective of increasing transparency, issued a preliminary report on National Treatment that presented the results of a survey of government measures in effect in Member countries that relate to National Treatment. The Committee found through that exercise that certain aspects of the scope and coverage of the instrument needed to be clarified in order to assist Member countries in applying it and to provide an improved basis for future surveys. The Committee thus had engaged in a programme of work which has led it to issue several clarifications of the instrument, some of which have already appeared in other OECD publications (4). This present publication brings together those clarifications to provide a comprehensive overview of the scope and coverage of the National Treatment instrument. Chapter II contains a number of explanations of the procedures to be undertaken for reporting by Member countries of measures related to National Treatment and for the review by the Committee of such measures. Chapter III provides certain general clarifications of the scope and meaning of the instrument. Chapter IV starts by presenting a classification of the different categories of measures relating to National Treatment and then gives a number of particular clarifications of the application of the instrument to these categories.

These clarifications of the instrument provided the basis for undertaking, in 1983, an augmented and updated survey of Member country measures related to National Treatment and an assessment of the relative importance of their effects on foreign investment. The results of this survey are presented in chapter V, and Annex II provides a detailed tabulation of the relevant Member country measures.

Chapter I

THE TEXTS OF OECD'S NATIONAL TREATMENT INSTRUMENT

1.1.   The National Treatment instrument consists of a section of the 1976 Declaration and a corresponding Council Decision.   The relevant texts are reproduced below.   The full texts of the 1976 Declaration and related Decisions can be found in Annex I.

A. EXCERPT FROM THE DECLARATION ON INTERNATIONAL INVESTMENT AND MULTINATIONAL ENTERPRISES
(21st June 1976)

THE GOVERNMENTS OF OECD
MEMBER COUNTRIES

DECLARE:

National Treatment

II. 1. That Member countries should, consistent with their needs to maintain public order, to protect their essential security interests and to fulfil commitments relating to peace and security, accord to enterprises operating in their territories and owned or controlled directly or indirectly by nationals of another Member country (hereinafter referred to as "Foreign-Controlled Enterprises") treatment under their laws, regulations and administrative practices, consistent with international law and no less favourable than that accorded in like situations to domestic enterprises (hereinafter referred to as "National Treatment");

2. That Member countries will consider applying "National Treatment" in respect of countries other than Member countries;

3. That Member countries will endeavour to ensure that their territorial subdivisions apply "National Treatment";

4. That this Declaration does not deal with the right of Member countries to regulate the entry of foreign investment or the conditions of establishment of foreign enterprises.

B. SECOND REVISED DECISION OF THE COUNCIL ON
NATIONAL TREATMENT

THE COUNCIL,

Having regard to the Convention on the Organisation for Economic Co-operation and Development of 14th December 1960 and, in particular, to Articles 2 c), 2 d), 3 and 5 a) thereof;

Having regard to the Resolution of the Council of 28th November 1979 on the Terms of Reference of the Committee on International Investment and Multinational Enterprises and, in particular, to paragraph 2 thereof [C(79)210(Final)];

Taking note of the Declaration by the Governments of OECD Member countries of 21st June 1976 on National Treatment;

Having regard to the Revised Decision of the Council of 13th June 1979 on National Treatment [C(79)144];

Considering that it is appropriate to establish within the Organisation suitable procedures for reviewing laws, regulations and administrative practices (hereinafter referred to as "measures") which depart from "National Treatment";

Considering the Report on the Second Review of the 1976 Declaration and Decisions on International Investment and Multinational Enterprises [C/MIN(84)5(Final)];

On the proposal of the Committee on International Investment and Multinational Enterprises;

DECIDES:

1.   Measures taken by a Member country constituting exceptions to "National Treatment" (including measures restricting new investment by "Foreign-Controlled Enterprises" already established in their territory) in effect on 21st June 1976 shall be notified to the Organisation within 60 days after that date.

2.   Measures taken by a Member country constituting new exceptions to "National Treatment" (including measures restricting new investment by "Foreign-Controlled Enterprises" already established in their territory) taken after 21st June 1976 shall be notified to the Organisation within 30 days of their introduction together with the specific reasons therefor and the proposed duration thereof.

3.   Measures introduced by a territorial subdivision of a Member country, pursuant to its independent powers, which constitute exceptions to "National Treatment", shall be notified to the Organisation by the Member country concerned, insofar as it has knowledge thereof, within 30 days of the responsible officials of the Member country obtaining such knowledge.

4.   The Committee on International Investment and Multinational Enterprises (hereinafter called "the Committee") shall periodically review the application of "National Treatment" (including exceptions thereto) with a view to extending such application of "National Treatment". The Committee shall make proposals as and when necessary in this connection.

5.   The Committee may periodically invite the Business and Industry Advisory Committee to OECD (BIAC) and the Trade Union Advisory Committee to OECD (TUAC) to express their views on matters related to National Treatment and shall take account of such views in its periodic reports to the Council.

6.   The Committee shall act as a forum for consultations, at the request of a Member country, in respect of any matter related to this instrument and its implementation, including exceptions to "National Treatment" and their application.

7.   Member countries shall provide to the Committee, upon its request, all relevant information concerning measures pertaining to the application of "National Treatment" and exceptions thereto.

8.   This Decision shall be reviewed at the latest in six years. The Committee shall make proposals for this purpose as appropriate.

9.   This Decision shall replace Decision [C(79)144].

Chapter II

IMPLEMENTATION PROCEDURES FOR THE NATIONAL TREATMENT INSTRUMENT

2.1.   The basic procedures for the implementation of the National Treatment instrument within the OECD are given in the Second Revised Decision of the Council on National Treatment, the text of which is presented in the preceding chapter.   The present chapter draws together a number of explanations of these procedures and their further development by OECD's Committee on International Investment and Multinational Enterprises (CIME) which is responsible for the implementation of this instrument.

2.2.   Reporting by Member countries of measures related to National Treatment

a) Paragraph 1 of the Decision called for the notification to the OECD within 60 days after 21st June 1976 of all meaures taken by a Member country "constituting exceptions to "National Treatment" (including measures restricting new investment by "Foreign-Controlled Enterprises already established in their territory").   The clarifications developed by the Committee, that are presented in chapters III and IV, were designed to assist Member countries to fulfil this requirement by establishing a common understanding of certain aspects of the scope and coverage of the instrument.

b) There are three further paragraphs of the Decision which relate to the reporting of measures by Member countries constituting exceptions to National Treatment.   Paragraph 2 of the Second Revised Decision provides that "measures taken by a Member country instituting new exceptions to National Treatment ... shall be notified to the Organisation within 30 days of their introduction together with the specific reasons therefor and the proposed duration thereof".   Paragraph 3 provides that "measures introduced by a territorial subdivison of a Member country pursuant to its independent powers, which constitute exceptions to National Treatment, shall be notified to the Organisation by the Member country concerned, insofar as it has knowledge thereof, within 30 days of the responsible officials of the Member country obtaining such knowledge".   Paragraph 7 provides that "Member countries shall provide to the Committee, upon its request, all relevant information concerning measures pertaining to the application of National Treatment and exceptions thereto".

c) The Committee has commented upon the basic reporting requirements in the Decision. The Committee considers the transparency and predictability of Government measures an important element for a favourable investment climate. Therefore, countries applying exceptions to National Treatment should state as clearly as possible the policies they pursue and the criteria they apply. (1979 Review Report, p.46). It would be desirable for Member countries to advise the Organisation of any actions taken to widen the scope of the application of National Treatment, i.e. relaxations in discriminatory treatment, so as to provide a clear picture of the current situation. (1979 Review Report, p.52). The process of focusing the attention of national administrations upon questions of National Treatment which has resulted from the Committee's activities with respect to this instrument should be beneficial in that it may lead to fresh consideration of the justification and the need for certain exceptions. (1979 Review Report, p.23).

d) The decision of the Committee to have Member countries report measures that do not constitute exceptions per se but result in restrictions on foreign-controlled enterprises, that was affirmed in connection with the 1983 survey, confirmed the scope of the reporting requirement. Measures to be reported for transparency include: those based on considerations of public order and essential security interests, those based on needs to maintain public commitments relating to international peace and security; restrictions on activities in areas covered by public monopolies; public aids and subsidies granted by the state as a shareholder or those designed to offset costs imposed by the state; restrictions that occur where the foreign-controlled firms may not be "in like situations" with respect to domestic firms. In particular, asset maintenance requirements for branches of foreign banks in host countries where different measures are applied to indigenous banks, measures relating to investments through established branches of foreign-controlled enterprises in host countries (see paragraph 4.5 c) infra), and nationality requirements for management or director positions in host countries are to be reported.

2.3. Review by the Committee of the application by Member countries of National Treatment and the consultation procedures

a) Paragraph 4 of the Second Revised Decision on National Treatment provides that the Committee "shall periodically review the application of National Treatment (including exceptions thereto) with a view to extending such application of National Treatment. The Committee shall make proposals as and when necessary in this connection". The substantial clarification work on the instrument that had been accomplished and the increased transparency of Member country measures and an assessment of the effects of such measures contained in the 1983 survey provided a basis for the Committee to focus its efforts in the 1984 Review Report on developing an approach for implementing paragraph 4 of the Second Revised Decision. It decided to undertake periodical in depth reviews of the major categories of measures related to National Treatment. The Committee recognised that such a category approach would no doubt require focusing on the countries that apply measures in the category under examination. During the periodic reviews, the Committee, if it so wished, would reach conclusions, possibly concerning specific countries. Such conclusions would be transmitted to the appropriate Delegations with the recommendation that they communicate with their authorities and report their authorities' reactions to the Committee. It was recognised that the Committee would also, when appropriate, in view of the objective of extending the application of National Treatment, report the results of its reviews to the Council accompanied by proposals as and when necessary in this connection. (1984 Review Report, p.47). The Committee also agreed to hold a thorough discussion each time a new exception is notified, including consideration of its motivation and proposed duration, although it would be unwise to place excessive attention on new exceptions compared to existing ones. In this context the Committee recalled that a consultation procedure is provided in paragraph 6 of the Second Revised Decision to discuss exceptions of particular importance, possibly new ones, if appropriate. (1984 Review Report, p.48).

b) In regard to the consultation procedure, the Committee has noted that under the procedures agreed in 1976 it was foreseen that the Committee should act at the request of a Member country as a forum for consultations in respect of any matter related to the National Treatment instrument and its implementation. A number of countries availed themselves of this possibility in 1980 regarding certain measures announced by another Member country (Mid-Term Report, p.23).

Chapter III

CLARIFICATIONS CONCERNING GENERAL ASPECTS OF THE INSTRUMENT

3.1.   In order to provide a basis for increased transparency of relevant government policies and measures and to assist governments in applying the instrument, the Committee has found it necessary to clarify the scope and extent of the National Treatment instrument. Transparency of Member countries' measures in this area is particularly important for foreign investors, as it will enable them to understand the treatment under laws, regulations and administrative practices to which they will be subject. Also, it assists the Committee in identifying the particular types of measures which deserve consideration in future work towards the objective of extending the application of National Treatment. The Committee's clarifications are also important for the determination of whether a particular measure is to be considered as an exception to National Treatment or not, and thus the extent to which the procedures in the National Treatment instrument and the related procedures established since 1976 apply to the measures in question. The clarifications contained in this chapter concern general aspects of the instrument. Clarifications relating to measures falling in a particular category, such as fiscal measures or government purchasing policies, are discussed in chapter IV.

3.2.   Public order and essential security interests

a) The National Treatment instrument states that "Member countries should, consistent with their needs to maintain public order, to protect their essential security interests ..., accord to ... foreign-controlled enterprises ... treatment ... no less favourable than that accorded in like situations to domestic enterprises". The Committee considered it necessary to clarify the implications of the provisions related to "public order" and "essential security interests". A review of concepts relating to public order and security in the legal systems of Member countries showed that, in general, there is no explicit definition of these concepts; rather, their interpretation depends on the specific context in which they are applied and may evolve over time according to changing circumstances. Also it was found that clauses relating to "public order" and "essential security interests" are frequently included in bilateral treaties or multilateral instruments relating to economic cooperation such as the OECD Codes of Liberalisation of Capital Movements and of Invisible Transactions, the EEC Treaty, or the GATT in order to qualify the obligations of the contracting parties. There also, no standard definition of these terms is given. (Mid-Term Report, p.70).

15

b) Given the experience with other international instruments and the wide variety of national practices, the Committee did not find it appropriate to seek a common definition of the terms "public order" and "essential security interests". The interpretation of these terms, therefore, should be left to Member countries. It was agreed, however, that the provisions relating to these terms should be applied with caution, bearing in mind the objectives of the National Treatment instruments; they should not be used as a general escape clause from the commitments under these instruments. (Mid-Term Report, p.70).

3.3. Operating in their territory

The National Treatment instrument calls for treatment by a host government of foreign-owned or controlled enterprises operating in their territory comparable to that accorded to locally-owned enterprises that are in like situations. The term "operating in their territory" in the instrument is meant to convey the concept of doing business from a place of business in the host country, as distinguished from conducting business in the country from abroad. While Member country practices differ regarding recognised forms of business organisations, the main forms of doing business in a host country for foreign-controlled enterprises are through locally-incorporated subsidiaries of foreign companies and through branches of foreign companies. There are other forms as well, such as sales offices and representative offices (5).

3.4. Owned or controlled

The Committee has determined that in considering the significance of the link between foreign ownership or control of an enterprise and National Treatment, control is the key factor. The criteria for determining control vary among Member countries and can include equity ownership, voting rights, power to appoint directors or otherwise influence the affairs of an enterprise.

3.5. Treatment no less favourable than that accorded in like situations to domestic enterprises

a) The Committee considered it necessary to clarify what was meant in the National Treatment definition by "treatment .... no less favourable than that accorded to domestic enterprises" in cases where domestic enterprises do not all receive the same treatment, and also to clarify the expression "in like situations". With regard to the first expression, the Committee, first of all, agreed that possible discriminatory measures deriving from the existence of a public monopoly were not deemed to be exceptions to National Treatment. The Committee considered the situations in which all domestic enterprises in a Member country were subject to the same treatment. It agreed that if a foreign-controlled enterprise already established in that Member country received less favourable treatment, this could constitute an exception to National Treatment and would do so if the other conditions determining these exceptions were fulfilled. If the enterprise under foreign control received treatment at least as favourable as domestic enterprises, there could be no case of an exception to National Treatment. (Mid-Term Report, p.67).

b) In situations in which domestic enterprises in a Member country did not all receive the same treatment, the Committee agreed that if a foreign-controlled enterprise already established in that Member country received less favourable treatment than the least well treated domestic enterprise, this could constitute an exception to National Treatment and would do so if the other conditions determining these exceptions were fulfilled. If the enterprise under foreign control received treatment at least as favourable as the best treated domestic enterprise, the Committee agreed that there could be no case of an exception to National Treatment. Finally, in cases where the enterprise under foreign control received treatment at least as favourable as the least well treated domestic enterprise but less favourable than the best treated domestic enterprise, the Committee considered that it was neither possible nor desirable to provide an answer of principle to the question of whether this could constitute an exception to National Treatment, even if the other conditions serving to determine such exceptions were fulfilled. The Committee agreed that the measures concerned in the latter cases should be examined pragmatically, in particular, taking into account individual national characteristics in this regard and the degree to which the foreign-controlled enterprise and the domestic enterprise concerned were placed in the same circumstances. In the interests of transparency and to enable the examination of the measures concerned in the manner mentioned above, the Committee agreed that Member countries should notify the Organisation of these measures in the same way as for exceptions to National Treatment, if the other conditions determining exceptions to National Treatment were met by the measures. (Mid-Term Report, p.67).

c) As regards the expression "in like situations", the Committee, first of all, agreed that comparison between treatment of foreign-controlled enterprises already established in a Member country and domestic enterprises in that Member country, in order to determine whether a measure taken by that Member country is discriminatory and could therefore constitute an exception to National Treatment, is valid only if the comparison is made between firms operating within the same sector. The Committee also agreed that more general considerations, such as the policy objectives of Member countries in various fields, could be taken into account in order to define the circumstances in which comparison between foreign-controlled and domestic enterprises is permissible inasmuch as those objectives are not contrary to the agreed principle of National Treatment. The Committee considered that, in any case, the real key to determining whether a discriminatory measure applied to foreign-controlled enterprises constitutes an exception to National Treatment was to ascertain whether the discrimination implied by that measure was actually motivated, at least in part, by the fact that the enterprises concerned are under foreign-control. The Committee also considered it useful to emphasize that use of the provision offered by the expression "in like situations" should be sparing and not excessive, in other words, extensive to the point of negating the spirit of the Declaration on National Treatment. Finally, the Committee considered that in the interests of transparency Member countries should notify the Organisation of any discriminatory measures applied to foreign-controlled enterprises, even if it was not established a priori that they would constitute exceptions to National Treatment. (Mid-Term Report, p.68).

3.6. Reciprocity

a) The principle of National Treatment, whereby equal treatment is to be accorded to both foreign-controlled and domestic enterprises by a host country, applies regardless of the home country's treatment of enterprises from the host country. It is true that the denial of National Treatment in a particular case based on reciprocity, whereby favourable treatment is accorded to a foreign-controlled enterprise only if the home country of such enterprise accords the same treatment to host country enterprises, usually reflects a different motivation from other restrictive measures covered by the instrument. The country in question may feel that by not allowing a foreign-controlled firm to engage in certain business activities unless its home country affords equal treatment to host country firms, it will encourage other countries to liberalise their treatment of foreign-controlled firms in general or at least their treatment of host country firms.

b) Nevertheless, one reason for allowing foreign-controlled firms to engage in business on the same basis as domestic firms is that the benefits of an additional competitor are what they are, regardless of whether the home country of that firm provides equal treatment to host country firms. Moreover, denial of National Treatment because of reciprocity considerations is at variance with multilateral approaches to international economic relations, as embodied, in particular, in the OECD instrument on National Treatment and constitutes an exception to National Treatment if it results in enterprises controlled by OECD Member countries' nationals being treated less favourably than domestic enterprises in a Member country.

c) Accordingly, certain exceptions to National Treatment included in the survey involve the application of reciprocity considerations by host countries. Under these measures the enterprises of some Member countries are accorded National Treatment, those from countries that meet the reciprocity conditions. But the measures are exceptions because not all Member countries' companies are accorded National Treatment in the cases in question. This is the case, for example, in this case of certain exceptions involving restrictions on the ability of foreign-controlled airlines to carry passengers from one national point to another. Some host countries permit some foreign-controlled airlines such privileges if the home country of the airline provides certain domestic routes to the host country's airlines. Exceptions involving reciprocity considerations also arise in the area of banking, both at the federal and territorial subdivision levels. Banking activities by foreign-controlled companies are permitted in some cases only if the home country allows host country companies similar privileges. Where Member countries have submitted that an exception is based upon reciprocity, this is noted under the motivation column in Annex II to the survey of Member country measures.

3.7. The entry of foreign investment and the scope of the National Treatment instrument

Paragraph 4 of the instrument indicates that this Declaration does not deal with the right of Member countries to regulate the entry of foreign investment or the conditions of establishment of foreign enterprises. Thus, conditions related to the initial investment and establishment in a country, i.e., by an enterprise that is not already established in the country concerned, are not covered by the National Treatment instrument. Initial foreign direct investments, i.e. investment by non-residents, are covered by another OECD instrument, the Code of Liberalisation of Capital Movements (6). Taken together, this Code and the National Treatment instrument cover fully the area of investment controls. The situation is different as concerns establishment, as on the other hand, further investment and establishment (in the same or other sectors or regions for instance) by established foreign-controlled companies (residents) are clearly covered by the National Treatment instrument, while, until recently, regulations on first establishment of foreign non-resident enterprises were not covered by the Capital Movements Code. However, the Council has now adopted a proposal by the Committee on Capital Movements and Invisible Transactions (CMIT), competent on all matters relating to the Capital Movements Code, that certain aspects of establishment regulations, i.e. measures raising special barriers or limitations to the access of non-resident (as compared to resident) investors to the operations of enterprises, that thereby prevent or significantly impede foreign direct investment should, in the future, be covered by the Capital Movements Code. Special efforts were made by both the CIME and CMIT to ensure the consistency and completeness of the respective approaches bearing in mind the specific characteristics of the respective instruments (National Treatment and the Capital Movements Code). The relationship between the two instruments is now defined in a precise manner allowing the very close co-operation between the two Committees to be pursued.

Chapter IV

CLARIFICATIONS CONCERNING PARTICULAR CATEGORIES OF MEASURES

4.1.   In its survey and analysis of measures relating to National Treatment
the Committee has found it useful to consider the application of National
Treatment in five main areas: official aids and subsidies, tax obligations,
goverment purchasing and public contracts, investment by established foreign-
controlled enterpises and access to local bank credits and the capital
market.   These are indeed the principal areas where Member countries' laws,
regulations and practices sometimes have a discriminatory effect on foreign-
controlled enterprises.   An additional area, that of nationality requirements
has also proved to be worth considering.   The Committee has issued a number of
clarifications of the measures referred to in the corresponding categories in
order to better delineate the scope of the instrument in these areas. Excerpts
and summaries of these clarifications are set forth in sections 4.2 to 4.7
below.   Used together with general clarifications discussed in chapter III
above, these more specific clarifications discussed in the present chapter
enabled countries to determine which measures are to be reported to the
Organisation and have assisted the Committee in implementing the National
Treatment instrument.

4.2.   Official aids and subsidies

a) The Committee considered that, in view of the possibility that
governments might discriminate in the provision of aids and subsidies to enterprises on the basis of nationality of ownership, this
area should be analysed to identify possible exceptions to National
Treatment (Mid-Term Report, p.69).   All Member countries practice
some degree of subsidisation but there exists a wide variance among
individual countries' practices and policies.   The Committee, therefore, felt it advisable to issue a clarification on the application
of National Treatment with respect to official aids and subsidies.
This clarification includes considerations relating to section 3.5
above, regarding a comparison between the situation of locally-owned
and foreign-controlled enterprises, in particular in cases when the
state is a shareholder of a locally-owned enterprise and when the
state imposes costs on enterprises and official aids and subsidies
are extended to such enterprises.

b) Accordingly, it was agreed to specify clearly the types of official
aids and subsidies which might constitute exceptions to National

Treatment. The following classification of official aids and subsidies was made:

i) Aids and subsidies granted by the State as a shareholder

This category covers:

-- The initial subscription to the capital of an enterprise;

-- State participation in a capital increase;

-- Surrender by the State of return on capital invested in an
enterprise;

-- Cover of operating losses.

ii) Official aids and subsidies designed to offset a particular
cost imposed by the State itself

In certain cases the State may seek to further its economic and
social policies through its management of public enterprises or
supervision of private enterprises. This may impose specific
burdens on these enterprises. Such costs are sometimes offset
by aids or subsidies which are designed to protect the viability of these enterprises.

iii) Aids provided bt the State as supplier of funds

This category includes external aids to enterprises of a financial or non-financial nature and which are granted by the State
in connection with its counter-cyclical, industrial, sectoral,
regional and other policies; it includes grants, low-interests
loans, interest subsidies and State guarantees. (Mid-Term
Report, p.69).

c) It was considered that measures in category iii) might be more
likely to entail exceptions to National Treatment than measures in
categories i) and ii). Although most measures in categories i)
and ii) would not be exceptions to National Treatment as a general
rule, some of the measures in category i) might constitute exceptions in specific circumstances. (Mid-Term Report, p.70).

4.3. Tax obligations

In applying the National Treatment instrument to fiscal measures, the
key consideration is, in general, whether a specific tax treatment is less
favourable to foreign-controlled enterpriss than to domestic enterprises in
like situations. It is therefore important to establish in each instance the
proper level of comparison between domestic and foreign-controlled enterprises. Residence is the factor which usually determines tax liability, and
tax administrations should not interpret National Treatment as meaning that
residents and non-residents should receive identical tax treatment. Nevertheless reference should also be made to the OECD Model Double Taxation Convention which gives further indications on this issue in its Article 24 dealing
with non-discrimination (7).

21

It should also be borne in mind that the application of National Treatment in the area of taxation may raise complex issues due to the fact that the interests of governments in an equitable sharing of the tax base between the country of source and the country of residence are involved, and that there is a legitimate concern to prevent tax evasion through the particular transfer pricing facilities available to international groups of affiliated enterprises. Furthermore, account has to be taken of the considerable network of bilateral tax treaties governing these matters.

It was considered important to make the following clarifications in relation to National Treatment and fiscal measures:

a) Imputation systems

These systems, by granting tax credits or refunds to resident shareholders (whether or not they are nationals of the country) for all or part of the corporation tax attributable to their dividends, are designed to reduce economic double taxation of a company's income. An issue was raised as to whether, under National Treatment, foreign non-resident shareholders should be entitled to the same credits or refunds as resident shareholders. The OECD's Committee on Fiscal Affairs has considered this problem but did not reach a conclusion as to whether the non-payment of such tax credits to non-resident shareholders, especially parent companies, constituted discrimination.

In order to establish the proper level of comparison between domestic and foreign-controlled enterprises, it could be argued that imputation systems operate at the level of the ultimate shareholder whereas companies are taxed alike. On the other hand, the denial of tax refunds to foreign parent companies could be seen to expose an international group of affiliated enterprises to a higher tax burden as compared to domestic groups and therefore might prove to be an impediment for the operation of foreign-controlled enterprises. As this result, however, could be avoided if the country of residence of the parent company provided a total or partial credit for the corporation tax borne by the subsidiary abroad, the issue of an equitable tax sharing between the country of source and the country of residence does arise. As remarked by the Fiscal Affairs Committee, such issues implying mutual concessions by the countries concerned can be resolved in the framework of bilateral treaties (8), or they can also be resolved by allowing different tax rates for distributed and undistributed profits. Therefore it would appear difficult to give a clear-cut answer which would be applicable in all circumstances. When everything is fully considered, it seems that the problem can be best solved in bilateral negotiations, where one is better placed to evaluate the sacrifices and advantages which bilateral treaties must bring for each contracting state.

b) International allocation of central group costs

The burden of proof imposed by tax authorities for allowing the allocation of central group costs has been dealt with in the Fiscal Affairs Committee's Report on Transfer Pricing and Multinational Enterprises (9). As it is stated in that report, what could be regarded as satisfactory evidence depends largely on the type of services rendered and on the circumstnces of each individual case. In order to substantiate the allocation of central expenditure of a multinational enterpise, the taxpayer should be prepared, in particular, to submit information about the structure and organisation of the enterprise and the functions and responsibilities of its component entities. Although this may imply a greater effort on behalf of larger enterprises, in particular, multinational enterprises, it results from this report that an increase in the burden of proof in order to prevent tax evasion cannot be considered to constitute discrimination against foreign-controlled enterprises. National Treatment could be seen to be involved if in similar circumstances, undue or unreasonable burdens were imposed on foreign-controlled enterprises as compared with domestic firms. However, reference should also be made to the first OECD Guideline on Taxation, which states:

"Enterprises should

> upon request of the taxation authorities of the countries in which they operate, provide, in accordance with the safeguards and relevant procedures of the national laws of these countries, the information necessary to determine correctly the taxes to be assessed in connection with their operations, including relevant information concerning their operations in other countries;"

c) International dividend taxes

This matter, again, involves maintaining an acceptable balance in sharing the tax base between the country of source and the country of residence and avoidance or limitation of double taxation which could emerge as a result. Article 10 2) of the OECD Model Double Taxation Convention puts forward recommendations in this regard. The fact that not all Member countries have followed these recommendations, does not in itself constitute a departure from National Treatment. The proper level of comparison is not between the foreign-controlled subsidiary and a domestic parent but between the foreign-controlled and a domestic subsidiary in like situations. Withholding taxes on dividends reduce the return of the ultimate shareholder on his invested capital only to the extent that he does not receive a tax credit from his country of taxation and do not directly affect the taxes borne by the subsidiary itself. Withholding taxes, by their nature, are anticipatory payments of the tax finally due and the incomplete elimination of double taxation, though regrettable and contrary to the principles of the OECD Model Convention, cannot be assimilated to a denial of National Treatment.

d) Fiscal Units

Tax treatment of affiliated enterprises as a single fiscal unit, or other forms of consolidated taxation granted as exceptions to the principle of separate taxation of each entity are generally designed to avoid economic double taxation of corporate profits and imply the possibility of off-setting gains and losses between affiliated enterprises at the national level (10). The addressees of these measures are parent companies as representing the group as a whole and, therefore, the proper level of comparison for the purpose of National Treatment is between domestic and foreign parents. For tax purposes these entities do not appear to be in a comparable situation, as domestic parent are subject to unlimited domestic corporate taxation on their total income including that derived from their subsidiaries, whereas foreign parents are generally not liable to such taxation in the host country. This consideration also applies to the so-called affiliation privilege which as a general rule is limited to domestic enterprises.

e) Unitary tax systems

Though such systems do introduce an irritant in the taxation of international investment and may result in taxation not in accord with internationally accepted principles of taxation of income from such investment (11), insofar as they do not impose a greater burden on foreign-controlled corporations than that on domestic-controlled corporations they are not contrary to National Treatment. The inclusion of factors relating to foreign corporations in the unitary tax base may result in distortions in the assessment of income for tax purposes. These factors, however, are present whether the controlling corporation of the group is domestic or foreign.

f) Tax treatment of loans by foreign parent companies

This matter has been considered by the Fiscal Affairs Committee in its Report on Transfer Pricing and Multinational Enterprises. Recognising the legitimate concern of tax authorities to prevent the use of loans as disguised equity contributions for purposes of tax evasion, the report discusses several approaches to dealing with this matter. Although a "multiple criteria test" making allowance for each specific situation was considered preferable, other methods such as the application of debt-equity ratios were not rejected as unreasonable or unacceptable. It would therefore be difficult to qualify such rules as inherently discriminatory to foreign-controlled enterprises other than in very exceptional circumstances. There is a diversity of rules and thresholds in this area in Member countries but such differences do not constitute exceptions to National Treatment.

g) Pension contributions

Although existing restrictions to the deductibility of contributions to pension funds located outside the national territory seem to apply to both domestic and foreign-controlled enterprises, they may constitute a special burden for the latter in view of the mobility of employees within multinational enterprises. This matter raises complex issues for international tax law given the diversity of pension systems and the tax treatment of contributions and benefits in various countries. There are differences which could be argued to justify a difference in the tax treatment of the contributions. While the host country knows that the pensions of domestic residents would normally be taxed in that country, this would not normally be the case with the pensions of employees of foreign firms retiring abroad. It was pointed out that the mobility of these employees causes difficulties and makes it unclear to see how National Treatment could be applied. However, there is agreement that the issue of pension contributions does pose serious taxation questions and the matter is to be discussed in the Committee on Fiscal Affairs.

4.4. Government procurement

a) Discriminatory procurement practices constitute important areas of exceptions to National Treatment. The public supply markets are an important source of income for particular sectors and a number of specific problems relating to possible departures from National Treatment in the field of government purchasing are often mentioned, including, inter alia, insufficient transparency of bidding procedures and preferential treatment for domestic as opposed to foreign-controlled enterprises in certain sectors. (Mid-Term Report, p.76).

b) The importance attached by governments to procurement practices is underlined by the considerable efforts which have been undertaken in this respect at the international level -- the National Treatment instrument of the OECD Declaration, the GATT Code on Procurement Practices and the activities of the EEC. There are important differences in the geographical coverage and, particularly, in the scope of application of these various efforts. In order to clarify the scope of application of the OECD National Treatment instrument, the Committee has found it necessary to point out these differences. For this purpose, three types of discriminatory practices should be distinguished:

   i) Discrimination against products and/or services supplied by a non-resident foreign enterprise;

   ii) Liberal policies towards procurement of imported goods and/or services but discrimination against bids submitted by locally established foreign-controlled enterprises;

   iii) Preferential treatment for local production and/or services supplied by domestic firms excluding both foreign and locally established foreign-controlled enterprises. (Mid-Term Report, p.76).

c) It is possible in most instances to draw a clear distinction as to the scope of application of the GATT Code and the EEC Directives on one side and the National Treatment instruments on the other. Procurement of imported products from non-resident enterprises would be covered by the GATT Code, but would not fall within the scope of National Treatment. If there is discrimination against locally established foreign-controlled enterprises but not against non-resident firms, only the National Treatment instrument would apply. If preference is given to domestic firms in exclusion of foreign competitors and locally established foreign-controlled enterprises, both the GATT Code (and within the Common Market the EEC Procurement Directives) and National Treatment would be relevant. However, since national practices vary with respect to the determination of the origin of products, there is uncertainty in some areas as to the application instrument. Therefore, depending on national practices, the supply of goods by locally established foreign-controlled enterprises may fall either under the GATT Code or under National Treatment. Whenever the rules of origin are such as to qualify goods or services offered by foreign-controlled enterprises as imported ones, the GATT Code applies; if these products or services are qualified as domestic ones, National Treatment under the OECD instruments is relevant. On the other hand pressures on foreign enterprises to establish local production in order to have access to government contracts do not seem to be covered by National Treatment. (Mid-Term Report, p.78).

d) Discrimination effected through the invisible use of administrative practices in the absence of clear procurement rules is one of the major obstacles to liberalisation of government purchasing. A lack of transparency, while not constituting per se an exception of National Treatment, may impose particular burdens on foreign-controlled enterprises to the extent that these enterprises are less familiar than domestic ones with the operations of national administrative procedures. This is one of the major concerns expressed by business in this area; and in this respect, compliance by governments with the transparency rules of the GATT Code and the EEC Directive is of interest not only to foreign producers but also for locally established foreign-controlled enterprises. In relation to National Treatment the Committee has requested that Member countries take account of the clarifications on the issue of government procurement in completing their notifications, especially since notifications reflecting publicly available laws and regulations may not provide an adequate picture of the actual situation. (Mid-Term Report, p.78).

e) A final issue requiring consideration in this area is the applicability of National Treatment instruments to the purchasing practices of public enterprises. The GATT Code applies only to listed entities at the central government level. The EEC Directives also cover regional and local authorities but exclude decentralised public enterprises, whether or not they have public or private law status. This is an important limitation since in some sectors, such as public services, governments often act through the intermediary of public enterprises. Under the 1976 Declaration, National Treatment applies only to government (central, state, local) action through laws, regulations and administrative practices, but it has been argued that the same principle should also apply where public enterprises are closely associated with government action, for instance through public monopolies or where discriminatory practices are taken by these enterprises on government instruction. The Committee did not reach a conclusion on this issue. (Mid-Term Report, p.79).

4.5. Investments by established foreign-controlled enterprises

a) As was noted in paragraph 3.7 above, the National Treatment instrument, calling for a non-discriminatory treatment of the operations of a foreign-controlled enterprise after it is established in the host country, can be seen as a complement to the obligations of the

26

Capital Movements Code, which relate to investments by non-residents, and does not supercede these obligations. During the drafting of the National Treatment instrument, the question arose whether investments made by foreign enterprises after their establishment in the host country should be considered as part of the operations of the enterprises covered by National Treatment or as representing the entry of new investment by non-resident sources and thereby falling under the Code. This question was settled in the Decision on National Treatment which states that exceptions under this instrument include measures restricting new investment by "foreign-controlled enterprises" already established in Member countries. Thus, the critical distinction is between investment by non-residents (covered by the Code of Liberalisation of Capital Movements) and investment by foreign-controlled enterprises already established in the host country. Although these two operations (inward foreign investments and investments by established foreign-controlled enterprises) may be seen separately in this way, in practice many countries apply the same laws, regulations or practices to both operations and, in such cases, the laws, regulations or practices may fall under both the Capital Movements Code and the National Treatment instruments.

b) When considering whether a measure affecting investment in a Member country by an enterprise under foreign control established in that country is to be considered as an exception to National Treatment, several issues need to be discussed in addition to those addressed in the preceding paragraph. They concern:

   i) The nature of the investing entity in question (subsidiary, branch, etc);

   ii) The type of investment (growth of the entity, extension, creation of a new entity, participation in or takeover of an existing entity, etc.);

   iii) The activities to be carried out through such investment, as such activities may be subject to specific regulations, or as regulations may concern the link between such activities and those already carried out in the country concerned by the investing entity;

   iv) In certain cases, the location of such investment (in areas that may be subjected to special legislation such as government lands, in territorial sub-divisions of the country concerned other than those of the original establishment, etc.).

The following paragraphs address these issues in the light of previous discussions of the Committee, and in relation to completed or ongoing work of the OECD Committee on Capital Movements and Invisible Transactions on the OECD Codes of Liberalisation.

c) The Council Decision on National treatment refers to new investment by "foreign-controlled enterprises already established (in their territory)". The interpretation of this last phrase is straightforward in cases when the investing entity is a foreign controlled

27

subsidiary operating in the country concerned, i.e. a locally-incorporated business entity with separate legal personality, generally regarded as a resident of the host country. If it meets the criteria of foreign control embodied in national legislation, it clearly comes within the definition of an established foreign-controlled enterprise. Accordingly, its investment activities fall within the scope of the National Treatment instrument. On the other hand, in the case of an additional investment by the parent company which is not carried out by an already established local affiliate, such additional investment would normally not fall under the National Treatment instrument, particularly if it is undertaken in a different, unrelated line of business. (Such investment would, however, fall under the Capital Movements Code as an inward investment by a non-resident). Conversely, an investment by a parent company undertaken by an established local affiliate would clearly be covered by the National Treatment instrument. In other words, the term "foreign-controlled enterprises already established in their territory" in the Decision refers to the domestic affiliates of the foreign parent companies and not to the (non-resident) parent companies themselves.

With respect to these distinctions, one additional point needs to be discussed concerning investments carried out by domestic branches of foreign enterprises operating in the country concerned. Branches are non-incorporated business establishments and are generally not considered as separate legal entities in the context of laws and regulations most relevant to investment or establishment. When carrying out direct investment activities, branches are, rather, considered as acting as agents of the foreign parent which is the beneficial owner of the facilities and the stock acquired. However, it is also recognised there are differences among various Member countries concerning company laws and regulations relating to establishment, and that distinctions between the status of subsidiaries and the status of branches may not always be clear cut. It has been argued that in particular cases the situation may be such that investments by parent companies abroad or by their foreign branches should be considered under the National Treatment instrument. For the purpose of transparency of Member countries' policies, and to ensure convergence in the interpretation of the scope of the National Treatment instrument, the Committee has recommended that measures restricting new investment by branches of foreign enterprises operating in their territories should also be reported by Member countries.

d) The OECD National Treatment instrument makes no reference as to the circumstances under which an operation by a foreign controlled enterprise already established (in their territory) is to be considered as (new) investment. Nevertheless such a reference was made in the Committee's 1978 Report on National Treatment suggesting that the following types of operations would appear to be covered by the National Treatment instrument, whether they are carried out, inter alia, through reinvested profits and local borrowing or with injection of fresh foreign capital:

-- Growth of the foreign-controlled enterprise;

-- Extension (by whatever techniques) in the same line of business or related area;

-- Creation of new activities (by fully-owned enterprises or joint ventures) in different lines of business;

-- Participation in or takeover of existing national enterprises.

This list of operations is generally consistent with the Capital Movements Code which considers the following list of means of investment:

-- Creation or extension of a wholly-owned enterprise, subsidiary or branch, acquisition of full ownership of an existing enterprise;

-- Participation in a new or existing enterprise;

-- A long-term loan (five years and longer).

These two references seem to deserve further comment. The fact that the National Treatment instrument does not refer to the means of new investment, in particular the way in which new investment is financed, should be taken as an indication that, whatever the means involved, the new investment operation should be considered as covered by the National Treatment Instrument.

e) The National Treatment instrument does not refer to the sectors or activities in which the new investment of foreign-controlled enterprises already established in the country concerned is made. As is the case for the question of the type of new investment operation discussed in section d) above, this should be taken as an indication that the instrument is intended to cover investments in all sectors of economic activity. Accordingly, many Member countries have notified exceptions relating to specific sectors where new investment by foreign controlled enterprises established in their territories is not treated equally to new investment by enterprises under national control, or where concessions and licences are not granted to foreign-controlled enterprises established in their territories on terms equal to those relating to enterprises under national control. On the other hand, the conditions of establishment of foreign-controlled enterprises that are not already established in the country concerned, are not covered by the National Treatment instrument.

f) In a number of countries, certain laws, regulations or practices may differ between geographical areas. This is the case for instance in countries with a federal or confederal institutional structure. It may also be the case in other countries implementing regional policies bearing on investment matters, or countries in which, for instance, local authorities are granted certain powers or in which government lands may be subject to specific legislation. In some countries, differences in laws, regulations and practices according to geographical areas include differences in rules of establishment. Furthermore, in certain cases, establishment may be granted only for a given geographical area, implying that an enterprise established in the geographical area concerned is not considered as established in another geographical area of the same country. The scope of the National Treatment instrument, and in particular its coverage of measures restricting new investment by foreign-controlled enterprise already established on a Member country's territory, needs clarification in these cases. It should first be noted that the Council Decision on National Treatment refers to measures taken by a Member country restriciting new investment by foreign-controlled enterprise established in (a Member country) territory, irrespective of the possible territorial subdivisions of that territory. The OECD Declaration on International Investment and Multinational Enterprises refers specifically to territorial subdivisions in its Section II.3, where it is stated: "Member countries will endeavour to ensure that their territorial subdivisions apply National Treatment". The issues that could be raised by that statement can be presented as follows:

-- Which measures are covered by Section II.3 of the Declaration rather than only by its more general Section II.1?

-- Are measures covered by Section II.3 of the Declaration, i.e., measures taken by territorial subdivisions of a Member country, to be considered as exceptions to National treatment?

With respect to the first issue, the term "endeavour to ensure" in Section II.3 of the Declaration would imply this section is intended to cover only the situations where a Member country government is not in a position to simply "ensure" that territorial subdivisions apply National Treatment. Section II.3 of the Declaration would only cover cases where territorial subdivisions are the basis of regulatory powers distinct from those of the national governments, and only areas of regulation where the relations between these regulatory powers and those of the national government are not such that these regulating powers are subordinated to those of national government. Thus, Section II.3 of the Declaration would refer for instance to states, provinces, cantons, municipalities, but not to national government lands; and it would cover the areas of legislation in which, for instance, the powers of states are not subordinated to those of the national government. As to the second issue, it should be recalled that the Committee, in its 1978 Report gave a positive answer and presented a number of such measures under its list of exceptions to National Treatment in the category "Investment by established foreign-controlled enterprises". Also, notifications of such exceptions are required by the Council Decision on National Treatment. The phrase "Member countries will endeavour to ensure" included in Section II.3 of the OECD Declaration, to be contrasted with the phrase "Member countries should" used in Section II.1 of that Declaration, should be taken as an indication that Member governmemts may not be in the same position when envisaging to reduce or eliminate exceptions relating to Section II.3 of the Declaration and exceptions concerning exclusively Section II.1 of the Declaration. The Council Decision also provides that measures introduced by a territorial subdivision of a Member country, pursuant to its independent powers, which constitute exceptions to "National Treatment", shall be notified to the Organisation by the

Member country concerned, insofar as it has knowledge thereof and the Committee has agreed that such measures are subject to review by the Committee.

4.6.   Access to local bank credit and the capital market

a) An important aspect of this matter concerns the position of foreign owned banks and other financial institutions in gaining access to funds of local origin, in particular deposits. The work so far stressed more the problems that could be met by foreign-owned non-financial companies in securing access to local credit. At the present time it appears that these problems do not require further clarification beyond that in paragraph f) below relating to preferential loans. In some Member countries, laws, regulations and practices exist which restrict the possibility for banks operating in the country concerned to open branches or agencies with the purpose of taking in deposits. Similar measures sometimes exist for other types of financial institutions, i.e., for instance, measures submitting to authorisation or restricting the possibility of insurance companies operating in the country concerned to set up branches or agencies with the purpose of canvassing. Such restrictive measures, for instance authorisation procedures where authorisation is not automatically granted after verification of the authenticity of the operation concerned, could be seen as restrictions to the access to that part of the local capital market consisting of domestic deposits. However, as a deposit operation in a bank also involves the bank concerned providing a service to the depositor and receiving a fee for that service, a bank's opening up of a new branch for the purpose of taking in deposits also represents an extension of the activities of that bank.

b) Where the measures concerned involve treatment of already established foreign-controlled banks less favourable than that of banks controlled by nationals in like situations, there is no doubt that they are covered by the National Treatment instrument to the same extent as any other type of discriminatory measure, i.e., with the qualifications to the obligations attached to the instrument agreed to in previous work of the Committee. To the extent that deposit operations are to be considered as involving the provisions of services by banks to the depositor, and at the same time providing the access of banks -- and more generally financial institutions -- to a section of the local capital market, the obligations and qualifications of the National Treatment instrument under both items "investment by established foreign-controlled enterprises" and "access to bank credit and the local capital market" would apply in the case of discriminatory laws, regulations, and practices restricting branching or similar activities of banks and of other financial institutions. The preceding analysis would imply, for instance, that the opening, by a foreign-controlled bank operating in a Member country, of additional branches for the purpose of collecting deposits, would be considered as new investment by the foreign-controlled bank concerned since it involves the provision of additional services by that bank, and the clarifications of the National Treatment instrument concerning new investment by foreign-controlled enterprises would apply to it. On the other hand, launching a borrowing activity by the foreign-controlled bank concerned by means that do not involve the provision of a service by that bank, for instance, obtaining a loan from another financial institution, would not be considered as involving the expansion of the activities of that bank. Thus, any measure affecting such loans, and discriminating against foreign-controlled banks (or enterprises) operating in the country concerned by means of imposing restrictions on the foreign-controlled banks in question (preventing them for instance from borrowing from certain domestic lenders) or on potential domestic lenders (i.e. imposing for instance on the latter restrictions as to their loans to foreign-controlled banks) would constitute an exception to National Treatment which falls under the category "access to bank credit and the local capital market".

c) The complex nature of the activities of financial institutions, for instance the fact that they engage in financial operations which often involve and sometimes automatically imply the provision of services, may in some cases raise other questions concerning the scope and coverage of the National Treatment instrument in relation to such measures as credit controls, lending requirements to certain sectors, requirements that banks' loan portfolios maintain a specified term structure, reserve requirements, etc. Two issues already appear to be be worth further consideration:

  i) Whether the measures concerned fall under the National Treatment instrument;

  ii) If the measures concerned fall under the National Treatment instrument, which categories of exceptions are concerned?

With respect to the first issue, it should be noted that the most important criterion for determining that a measure falls under the National Treatment instrument is that the measure grants to foreign-controlled enterprises operating in a Member country treatment "less favourable than that accorded in like situations to domestic enterprises". Thus for instance credit controls or ceilings, lending requirements to certain sectors and similar measures such as loan portfolio requirements or swap limits imply exceptions to National Treatment only if they would discriminate against foreign-controlled banks or financial institutions operating in a Member country vis-à-vis domestic banks or financial institutions in like situations, taking into account the position of foreign banks, which tend in many countries to be organised in branch rather than domestically incorporated subsidiary form. The question has also been raised of the extent to which such conditions relate to entry matters falling under the Capital Movements Code or in the area of establishment.

d) These considerations also apply to other measures, such as those imposing reserve requirements, deposits, or measures involving capital asset ratios, etc. Such measures, when they apply to foreign-controlled subsidiaries, i.e. enterprises incorporated under local law, would clearly be covered by the National Treatment instrument if they involve discrimination against the foreigncontrolled subsidiaries as compared to other enterprises incorporated under local law, i.e. domestic enterprises. But in attempting to determine whether such measures, where they apply to local branches of banks under foreign control, are to be considered as exceptions to National Treatment, the question arises as to whether the measures should be compared solely to measures applying to branches of banks under domestic control? Or should reference be also made to measures applying to other entities or enterprises under domestic control? In considering this question, it is useful to recall that measures imposing reserve requirements, special deposits etc. on foreign-controlled branches -- as opposed to foreign controlled subsidiaries or domestic enterprises -- often are motivated by the prudential objectives of the regulatory authorities, such as the safeguard of the interests of clients, to which local incorporation, at the national or state level, can be seen to contribute through the commitment represented by the capital stock involved in local incorporation, or through the fact that local incorporation implies direct access of the local or national legal system to the incorporated entity. However, local incorporation need not always be considered as indispensible in relation to these objectives. Taking these elements into account, the Committee considered that in attempting to determine whether measures such as those referred to in paragraph c) above, where they apply to local branches of banks under foreign control, are to be considered as exceptions to National Treatment, comparisons should not be limited to those with branches under domestic control. Account should also be taken of the specific circumstances applying in each case, relating, for instance, to elements which could be considered to contribute to the commitment of local branches under foreign control in a way comparable to the capital stock of domestic enterprises. The final answer should be guided by the principle according to which measures applying to local branches under foreign control are to be considered as exceptions to National Treatment if they amount to a treatment less favourable than that accorded in like situations to domestic enterprises.

e) Obviously, the importance of determining whether or not a measure is to be considered an exception to National Treatment is greater than that of the classification of such measures into the various categories of exceptions, even if in some cases this second issue may be significant insofar as different clarifications apply to the various categories. In the latter cases, and when a measure restricts simultaneously several inseparable activities of an enterprise that, nevertheless, relate to different categories of exceptions to National Treatment, the obligations and qualifications of the National Treatment instrument relating to the different categories of exceptions would apply. In other cases the classification issue may be immaterial. In such cases it may be that some measures are found difficult to classify in any single category.

f) A further issue relates to the access of foreign-controlled enterprises, whether financial or non-financial, operating in a Member country to special credit institutions, or special credit lines in the context of policies involving credit control. Measures restricting access of enterprises to such credit institutions or lines would be considered as exceptions to National Treatment if they would treat the foreign-controlled enterprises less favourably than domestic enterprises in like situations. Where the credits concerned are not provided at market prices, or at the conditions generally prevailing in the country concerned for the category of borrowers concerned, but involve government aids and subsidies, the discriminatory measures involved would relate to both categories of exceptions "government aids and subsidies" and "access to bank credit and the local capital market". As such the obligations and qualifications applying to both categories would apply. Where the credits concerned are provided at market prices or on the conditions generally prevailing in the country concerned for the category of borrowers concerned, the discriminatory measures involved would only relate to the category of exceptions "access to bank credits and local capital markets".

4.7. <u>Corporate organisation: nationality requirements</u>

The Committee considered measures which are directed at foreign-controlled and domestic enterprises alike but by their nature or their application may have different effects on foreign-controlled and domestic enterprises. The de facto discrimination which may result from the issuance and application of formally even-handed laws and regulations represents a difficult aspect of the application of the principle of National Treatment. An example mentioned in a number of notifications referred to nationality requirements providing for a majority participation of nationals of the host country in the management and/or the board of directors of an enterprise. Many Delegations doubted whether such requirements constitute exceptions to National Treatment, but it was agreed that they should be reported, nevertheless, in the general interest of transparency. (1979 Review Report, p.51).

Chapter V

SURVEY OF MEMBER COUNTRY MEASURES RELATED
TO NATIONAL TREATMENT

I. INTRODUCTION

5.1.   In 1978, the Committee on International Investment and Multinational Enterprises completed a first, preliminary survey of measures related to National Treatment (12).   On the basis of the progress since 1978, the Committee and its Working Group on International Investment Policies decided to engage in a comprehensive Member country survey of government measures considered to constitute exceptions to National Treatment, and of a number of measures that may not or do not constitute such exceptions but, nonetheless, are to be communicated to the Committee in the context of its work on National Treatment, and of governments' motivations for such measures.   The present chapter presents the results of that survey and assesses the relative importance of the impact of the identified measures on foreign investors.

5.2.   The main sources of information for the present survey were responses by Member governments to a questionnaire on measures related to National Treatment and the 1978 survey.   In addition, information obtained over the past two years in OECD documents has been utilised.   Among these, the published report of the CMIT, "Controls and Impediments affecting Inward Direct Investment in OECD Countries" should be singled out.

5.3.   Work in other committees of the OECD, and in particular work on trade in services, has also brought to light a number of measures related to National Treatment.   The advisory groups to the OECD have also been an important and growing source of information.   BIAC, the Business and Industry Advisory Committee of the OECD, undertook a comprehensive inquiry among its members and produced a report that has provided additional information about discriminatory practices related to foreign-controlled enterprises (13).   It presents the foreign investors' views as to the discriminatory practices they encounter and the economic importance of this discrimination.

5.4.   The present survey on National Treatment accordingly differs significantly from the earlier 1978 survey in several respects.   Much more information is available on measures related to National Treatment as compared to the earlier survey and this is for several reasons.   There is a better understanding of the concept of National Treatment because of the clarifications that have been issued related to categories of exceptions to National Treatment.

This has enabled countries to better identify which measures are to be reported and many measures are included in the present survey that were not included in the 1978 survey.

5.5.   In large part the more comprehensive coverage of this survey reflects the Committee's decisions in the course of its work on the clarifications discussed in chapters III and IV above that certain measures that may not fall within the scope of the National Treatment instrument should nevertheless be communicated to the Organisation for purposes of transparency (14). Measures to be reported for transparency (often referred to as transparency items below) include those based on needs to maintain public order, to protect essential security interests and to fulfill commitments relating to international peace and security (15), and restrictions on activities in areas covered by public monopolies (16). The Committee has also considered that public aids and subsidies granted by the state as a shareholder or those designed to offset costs imposed by the state (17), or restrictions that occur where the foreign-controlled firms may not be "in like situations" with respect to domestic firms were also to be reported for purposes of transparency even if they were not considered to constitute exceptions to National Treatment (18). In particular, measures relating to reserve requirements, deposits, etc. for branches of foreign banks in host countries where different measures are applied to indigenous banks, measures relating to investments through established branches of foreign-controlled enterprises in host countries, and nationality requirements for management or director positions in host countries (19) are to be reported even though they do not constitute exceptions to National Treatment. While the National Treatment Instrument addresses measures taken by government at all relevant levels (including territorial sub-divisions) (20), discriminatory policies and practices of government-sanctioned institutions are also to be reported for purposes of transparency.

5.6.   The Committee also believed it important that the survey seek to identify to the extent possible the motivations underlying the identified exceptions. OECD governments adopted the National Treatment principle in 1976 to increase international co-operation in the area of international investment. While the instrument is aimed at limiting as much as possible discriminatory restrictions on foreign-controlled companies so that they can contribute to economic growth, it is recognised that various motivations, reflecting, inter alia, the different traditions in Member countries, may lead in certain areas to differential treatment of such enterprises. The reported motivations, where available, for the identified exceptions to National Treatment are thus included in the survey results below.

5.7.   Given the above considerations, the resulting increase in the size of the report and the number of measures covered in comparison with the 1978 Report should not lead the reader to think that since 1978 exceptions to National Treatment have mushroomed in OECD Member countries. Rather, in the present survey results, the description of measures is often more extensive, the motivations for measures are also often included, and information regarding the administering authority, the automatic versus the discretionary administration, the duration of a measure and the results achieved are also included.

5.8.   Part II of the present chapter presents the main results of the survey, covering exceptions and other measures. It is organised according to five broad categories of exceptions (official aids and subsidies, tax obligations, access to local bank credit and the capital market, government purchasing and public contracts, investment by established foreign-controlled enterprises). Comments noting elements of clarifications on the scope of the instrument are provided when relevant, especially those that distinguish between exceptions and measures reported for purposes of transparency. Information concerning motivations for the measures discussed is reported when available. Part III of the present chapter presents additional remarks relating to the notion of public order and security and to international transportation that are useful to understand the results of the survey on these subjects, and more generally the Committee's approach and understanding of the scope of the instrument in the areas involved. Part IV presents the Committee's assessment of the relative importance of exceptions to National Treatment and other measures, which is examined in terms of their effects on foreign-owned firms. The complete results of the survey information on a country-by-country basis for each category of measures are included in tables in Annex II. These tables are obviously much more detailed and comprehensive than part II of the present chapter which considers only the most important elements emerging from the survey. Measures selected for discussion and for tabular presentation in part II are generally those which occur with some frequency among Member countries and those that apparently or potentially have a broad application or important impact on foreign investors.

II. CATEGORIES OF MEASURES

5.9. This section discusses measures related to National Treatment by categories, including both measures that are clear exceptions to National Treatment and measures which are to be reported for the purpose of transparency (transparency items) and the motivations underlying these measures. The main categories in which it was found useful to group these measures are (21):

a) Official aids and subsidies;

b) Tax obligations;

c) Access to local bank credit and the capital market;

d) Government purchasing and public contracts;

e) Investment by established foreign-controlled enterprises.

a) Official aids and subsidies

5.10. This category refers to official financial and other assistance (subsidies, credits on preferential terms, tax rebates) to business enterprises given for such policy reasons as demand management, employment and industrial policy, promotion of research and development, and regional development. The Committee has classified official aids and subsidies in three broad categories:

i) Public aids and subsidies granted by the state as a shareholder;

ii) Those designed to offset costs imposed by the state;

iii) Aids provided by the State as supplier of funds.

Categories i) and ii) are to be reported for transparency.

Aids and subsidies granted by the State as a shareholder cover: the initial capital subscription, participation in capital increases, reinvestment of profits, covering operating losses. Those designed to offset costs imposed by the state arise in cases where the state may seek to further its economic and social policies through its management of public enterprises or supervision of private enterprises which may impose specific burdens on these enterprises, and compensate for these burdens by public aids and subsidies. Aids provided by the State as a supplier of funds include external aids to enterprises granted by the State in various connections such as counter-cyclical, industrial, regional and other policies in the form of grants, loans, interest subsidies and guarantees. In its clarification on this subject, the Committee considered that official aids and subsidies granted by the state when it acts as supplier of funds would be more likely to entail exceptions to National Treatment than those in the other categories. It was also felt that the area of government aids and subsidies was one where transparency of government policies or administrative practices was most difficult to achieve, in particular in defence related areas or similar areas such as that of computer and telecommunications industries.

5.11. Exceptions under this category were found in twelve Member countries. In this category, measures are usually applied by governments to specific sectors of the economy rather than to many diverse sectors. A few examples may be cited. In Canada, the federal government provides grants for mineral exploration in Northern Canada, stabilization payments to grain producers, and grants for oil and gas exploration. The Canadian provinces of Alberta and Saskatchewan provide loans and grants, respectively, for agriculture. The United States has programmes for emergency loans for agricultural purposes and for foreign investment insurance. Certain countries favour specific sectors such as oil (Austria and Canada), film production (Greece, Italy and Switzerland), tourism (six countries -- see Table 1).

5.12. In regard to transparency items in this category, a few examples may be given. The United States, among other countries, maintains several measures regarding maritime transportation financing, shipping and construction that are based on national security. In Norway, the state-owned oil company enjoys certain preferences as a public monopoly. The United Kingdom provides certain subsidies for film production and one criterion for assistance is that the companies' central management and control is exercised in an EEC country, which would exclude branches of foreign-controlled companies from certain Member countries. Australia provides financial assistance to the film industry based on residency. Germany has a programme of assistance to the tourism industry that also excludes branches of foreign-controlled enterprises.

Table 1

OFFICIAL AIDS AND SUBSIDIES:
EXCEPTIONS

Oil companies -- preferential treatment related to grants for exploration or production (Canada) or for prices or supplies (Austria).

Branches of foreign companies ineligible for aids: Australia.

Financial assistance and guarantees for tourism: Finland, Iceland, New Zealand, Spain, Austria, Turkey.

Subsidies for film production: Greece, Italy, Switzerland.

Subsidies for mining: New Zealand.

5.13. In many countries, exceptions or other relevant measures in this category are motivated by the objective of encouraging locally-owned enterprises and/or preserving the infrastructure of production in a particular sector. For instance, assistance to the film industry in Switzerland and in the U.K. reflects these motivations. Canada provided motivations regarding discriminatory aids for oil and gas production, mineral exploration and for grain production. Canada has submitted that in each case the objective is to encourage Canadian-owned enterprises in these sectors and, in the extractive industries, to promote development of these mineral resources. Three Canadian provinces provide aids to commerce, publishing or agriculture, in each case to encourage Canadian-owned firms in these sectors. The United States provides discriminatory financial assistance (loans, guarantees or insurance) for agricultural programmes and foreign investments in each case to assure the availability of limited financial assistance to locally-owned firms.

b) Tax obligations

5.14. This is a complex area in which the Committee has, in co-operation with the Committee on Fiscal Affairs, provided clarification on the scope of the instrument (22). Avoidance of discrimination in this area is also promoted by the OECD Model Double Taxation Convention on Income and Capital, which is taken into account in the numerous bilateral tax treaties between Member countries. Particular reference is to be made to Article 24 of this Convention. Both this instrument and the National Treatment Instrument thus contribute to the same goal (23). Concerning the latter instrument, it should also be noted that fiscal measures amounting to aids and subsidies have been classified as aids and subsidies rather than as tax obligations.

5.15. An exception was reported by only one country under the item of tax obligations, undoubtedly because of the understanding referred to above. In two Canadian provinces, there are higher or special land transfer taxes for foreign-controlled corporations.

Table 2

TAX OBLIGATIONS:
EXCEPTIONS

Higher or special land transfer taxes for foreign-owned companies:
Canada (Ontario and Quebec provinces).

Table 3

TAX OBLIGATIONS:
TRANSPARENCY

Special tax for branches of foreign companies: Australia.

Branches of foreign companies subject to higher tax rate than locally
incorporated companies: Belgium, New Zealand.

Branches of foreign companies denied certain tax credits or deductions:
Belgium, Sweden.

5.16. With respect to transparency items in the category of tax obligations,
in Australia, Belgium, New Zealand and Sweden, branches are subject to higher
tax rates or additional taxes and/or denied certain tax credits or deductions
as compared to locally-incorporated companies, while the latter are subject to
other obligations, concerning for instance equity, that are not applicable to
branches. As branches in Australia, Belgium and Sweden owned indirectly by
nationals of those countries are subject to the same treatment as branches of
foreign-owned companies, there is no discriminatory treatment between these
two kinds of branches.

5.17. In regard to motivations, Canada reported that the higher or special
land transfer taxes for foreign-owned corporations in Ontario and in Quebec
are to encourage Canadian ownership of land in those provinces. Other motivations reported indicate that some measures result from the objective of comparable treatment of enterprises with different attributes. The denial of tax
credits for dividend withholding taxes for branches in Belgium is to attain
tax neutrality between branch and subsidiary forms of operations. In Sweden,
the denial of deductions from taxable income for branches of foreign companies
is an attempt at tax equalisation between branches and subsidiaries.

c) Access to local bank credit and the capital market

5.18 Exceptions in this category are present in six countries. Five countries apply limitations on access to local bank credit and the capital market
in general, while one country requires prior authorisation for loans guaranteed by a non-resident enterprise.

Table 4

ACCESS TO LOCAL BANK CREDIT AND THE CAPITAL MARKET:
EXCEPTIONS

Limitations on access to local bank credit or capital markets:
Ireland, Italy, New Zealand, Portugal, Spain.

Prior authorisation for loans guaranteed by non-resident enterprises:
Sweden.

5.19. These measures appear generally to have a common aim, namely to induce foreign-controlled enterprises to cover part of their internal financing requirements by borrowing from the parent company, or by borrowing from un-related parties abroad, or by capitalisation from the parent company, in order to increase foreign exchange receipts of the host country. The degree of restriction on local financing varies, in general, with the balance-of-payments position of the host country. Whether the resulting discrimination creates a burden for the foreign-controlled firm depends on the relative terms and conditions for borrowing in the host country and abroad and on exchange rate fluctuations.

5.20. Portugal confirmed that its motivation in restricting borrowing by foreign-controlled firms is to ensure that foreign investment is not financed predominantly from local bank credit. The same motivation is stated by Sweden in respect of its requirement for authorisation for loans with foreign guarantees.

d) Government purchasing and public contracts

5.21 Fourteen Member countries reported exceptions in this area. However, it should be noted that ten countries maintain an exception whereby government employees or employees of government companies are urged to use air and mari-time transportation services of national companies. Six countries maintain exceptions in other areas. In Portugal majority-locally-owned firms (there may be minority foreign interests) are generally favoured in public works con-tracts, although for electrical and mechanical equipment installation con-tracts, when solicitations for bids do not receive an adequate response, and if the nature of a project justifies such a measure, foreign-controlled firms may be awarded such contracts. In Germany, the post-office (DBP) purchases telecommunications equipment mainly from locally-owned firms. Australia, the U.K., and the U.S. have foreign aid programmes under which generally only locally-owned firms are awarded consultancy contracts.

5.22. Some countries have provided motivations for their exceptions in the category under examination. For instance, Australia, the U.K. and the U.S. provided as motivations for their restrictive consultancy programmes their desire to insure the capability of the consultants hired. Australia also indicated the objective of ensuring that Australian firms have the opportunity of participating in overseas development projects. In Portugal restrictions on public work contracts are motivated by reasons of public interest.

Table 5

GOVERNMENT PURCHASING AND PUBLIC CONTRACTS:
EXCEPTIONS AND TRANSPARENCY

Public works projects generally reserved to locally-owned firms:
Portugal.

Preferential treatment for locally-owned firms in defence sector:
Austria, France, U.S.

Government employees: required/urged to use national airlines/ferry
services: Canada, France, Germany, Greece, Italy, Netherlands, New
Zealand, Switzerland, Turkey, U.S.

Consultant firms retained for foreign assistance programmes must be
locally-owned: Australia, U.K., U.S. (some exceptions).

5.23. When countries cite national security interests or the public order as
reasons for discriminatory measures against foreign-controlled companies in
public purchasing, these measures are not considered as exceptions but rather
as measures reported for transparency. Such measures are frequently found in
Member countries, and provide the transparency items in the category under
examination. Three countries (Austria, France, United States) have indicated
that they accord preferential treatment to domestic enterprises based on
national security in the field of defence related contracts. In one country
these regulations are directly based on nationality and automatically exclude
competition by foreign or foreign-controlled enterprises except in cases of
co-production or intergovernmental agreements. In France, preferential treatment in government purchasing is given in the form of guaranteed orders or by
other means for locally-owned firms in sectors related to defence. In the
U.S., foreign-controlled enterprises need special arrangements to be awarded
defence procurement contracts involving classified information. Other countries have accorded preference in certain circumstances to domestic enterprises because of security requirements as these enterprises are considered
more able to meet the need for stability of supply. It appears that these
other measures or practices that are considered by the Member countries concerned as related to public order and essential security interests are rather
widespread in the OECD area and that further efforts should be devoted to increase transparency and administrative practices in this respect, in particular in relation to defence-related sectors or similar sectors like computers
and telecommunications. The issues relating to this question are discussed in
section III below.

e) Investments by established foreign-controlled enterprises

5.24. All Member countries reported exceptions in this field and, in fact,
the preponderance of the exceptions to National Treatment that were notified
fall under the category "investments by established foreign-controlled enterprises" (24). Some exceptions in this category relate to investments of
foreign-controlled enterprises regardless of the sector of business activity
concerned. The measures concerned generally relate to investment in new
plants or facilities in the same or unrelated business activities, takeovers

and real estate acquisition (25). Measures of a non-sector specific type have been reported by fourteen Delegations. Two countries (France and Norway) require that in certain cases investments by a foreign-controlled enterprise are subject to prior authorisation or notification (26). In France, in general, the establishment of a company by an established foreign-controlled company is subject to prior approval. With the exception of investments of less than FF 10 million per year, established foreign-controlled companies controlled by non-EEC interests are required to obtain prior authorisation for some other types of investments, while EEC-controlled enterprises must present a prior notification. In Norway, the expansion of existing investments by foreign-controlled enterprises must be approved and an established foreign-controlled company must have a concession to establish a new company or acquire a company. The granting of such a concession may be subject to conditions regarding parent-subsidiary pricing and technical assistance, and financing and production. In Finland, foreign-controlled enterprises must seek the prior authorisation of the government to engage in an activity outside its field of operation. In Australia, proposals for the establishment of a new business involving diversification into activities not previously undertaken by the foreign interest in Australia require approval. In Canada, the expansion by foreign-controlled companies into unrelated business activities, and all acquisitions of Canadian business enterprises, requires approval to determine whether there is significant benefit to Canada. In Japan, prior notification is required when foreign-controlled enterprises wish to change the activities of their business. In New Zealand, authorisation is required for expansion into non-related areas or for takeovers by established foreign-controlled companies. In Portugal, changes in the business activity of foreign-controlled companies as indicated in their articles of association and the acquisition of more than 50 per cent of the capital of another company are subject to prior approval.

5.25. In the area of acquisitions by foreign-controlled companies (in addition to requirements noted above in Canada, France, New Zealand, Norway and Portugal), Finland, Luxembourg, Spain and Sweden also have requirements. In Luxembourg, takeover bids by non-EEC controlled companies must be approved. In Spain, foreign-controlled enterprises that wish to control more than 50 per cent of a Spanish enterprise must apply for authorisation. In Sweden authorisation is required for proposed acquisitions by foreign-controlled corporations of shares in Swedish corporations exceeding certain levels of equity capital. A permit shall be granted if the acquisition is not in conflict with any essential public interest. In case any undertakings of importance to the decision have been made by the acquirer such undertakings shall be mentioned in the decision. Seven countries have requirements regarding authorisation for firms operating in any sector to acquire real estate and such a measure is considered a general rather than a sector-specific measure for the purposes of classification.

5.26. Measures in some countries relate to investments in particular sectors of the economy. Controls on new investments in specific sectors that constitute exceptions have been reported by all countries. The bulk of restrictions on the activities of foreign-controlled enterprises can be found in the following sectors:

    -- Air and/or maritime transportation: All countries

    -- Mining and/or natural resources: 9 countries

-- Banking and/or insurance: 18 countries

-- Radio and TV broadcasting and/or publishing: 8 countries

-- Agriculture and/or fishing: 7 countries

5.27. Measures of host countries relating to nationality requirements for managers and/or directors of companies are also found in Member countries. In addition to the requirements in the maritime transportation sector noted in paragraph 41 below, eight countries, Canada, Finland, France, Italy, Norway, Sweden, Switzerland and the United States reported nationality requirements. Among these Member countries, these requirements may apply to one or more sectors.

5.28. In this category, measures to be reported in the interest of transparency include the reservation of public services to the state. These measures are widespread among Member countries and include the state exclusively providing such services as railroad transportation, postal services and telecommunications. Perhaps because such measures are so prevalent, few countries have reported them. In regard to the insurance sector in the EEC, European Communities Directives establish uniform rules for solvency margins and the location of related assets for insurance companies of EEC countries. Branches and agencies of insurance companies of non-EEC countries cannot by their nature be subject to identical EEC rules and are subject to different financial solvency requirements which have comparable prudential objectives. Other transparency items in the present category, other than those based on national security, are relatively few.

5.29. In regard to motivations for measures in this category other than those based on national security, measures reported by eight countries (Australia, Belgium, Canada, Japan, Portugal, Sweden, U.K. and the U.S.) relate to general foreign investment policy considerations and to certain sectoral policies. The requirement for approval in Canada for acquisition of all Canadian enterprises and expansion of investments in non-related areas is to determine whether the investment proposal is likely to be of significant benefit to Canada. Similarly, authorisation for expansion in non-related areas in Australia is to ensure the consistency of the proposal with Australian interests. The prior notification requirement in Japan to engage in agriculture, fisheries, forestry, mining, the oil industry and leather products manufacture is for natural resources and employment policy. The requirement in Portugal for prior authorisation for certain investments is to survey the importance of foreign investment in Portugal. In Sweden, restrictions on foreign ownership of corporations are to protect essential public interests, restrictions that may be imposed on mining by foreign-controlled companies are to protect national resources, and restrictions on foreign ownership of banks are to limit foreign influence in this important sector. The provision of law in the U.K., whereby a proposed transfer of control of a manufacturing plant to a non-resident may be prohibited, is to safeguard national interests of the U.K. Takeover bids by non-EEC companies for Belgian public companies are subject to authorisation to consider the compatibility of the proposed acquisition with the state of the local financial market. Three countries, Canada, Finland and the U.S. provided motivations for restrictions on foreign-controlled enterprises' participation in mining and natural resources projects. In Canada, in regard to oil and gas operations, the objective is to increase energy security and to maximize the opportunities for Canadian controlled firms. In Finland, the measures attempt to maintain natural resources under domestic control. In the United States, the intent of the federal law relating to the granting of interests in leases on federal on-shore territory is to promote reciprocity in foreign countries, while the restrictions imposed by a few states in the United States are to limit access to U.S. citizens and also for reciprocity. The Netherlands provided motivations for its restrictions on foreign ownership of ships that fly the national flag and of aircraft licensed to operate in the Netherlands. These measures, which are found in many other countries as well, are maintained in the Netherlands to ensure compliance with Dutch safety standards and laws pertaining to social security, taxation and industrial relations. Measures motivated by public order and essential security interest considerations are discussed below in section III.

Table 6

INVESTMENTS BY ESTABLISHED FOREIGN-CONTROLLED ENTERPRISES

A. General Measures

1.   Authorisation or notification required for expansion of investment in any field: France (for some investments), Norway.

2.   Authorisation required for expansion in non-related areas: Australia, Canada, Finland, Japan (prior notification), New Zealand, Portugal.

3.   Authorisation required for or restrictions on takeovers: Canada, Finland, France, Luxembourg, New Zealand, Norway, Portugal, Spain, Sweden.

4.   Restrictions on acquisition of real estate: Austria, Finland, Greece, New Zealand, Norway, Sweden, U.S..

B. Sectoral Restrictions

5.   Restrictions on engaging in banking or financial services: Australia, Austria, Canada, Finland, France, Germany, Greece, Italy, Netherlands, New Zealand, Norway, Spain, Sweden, Switzerland, Turkey, U.K., U.S.

6.   Restrictions in insurance: Australia, Canada, France, Italy, Netherlands, Norway, Portugal, Sweden, Switzerland.

7.   Restrictions on broadcasting and/or publishing: Australia, Canada, Finland, France, Japan, Portugal, Spain, U.S.

8.   Restrictions in mining and/or natural resources: Australia, Canada, Finland, Greece, Japan, Portugal, Spain, Sweden, U.S.

9.   Restrictions in oil and/or gas industry (e.g. exploration and production): Canada, Japan, U.S.

10.   Restrictions on investment in agriculture and/or fishing: Finland, France, Ireland, Japan, Norway, Portugal, U.S.

11. Restrictions on ownership of ships registered in the country in question: Austria, Finland, France, Germany, Greece, Iceland, Italy, Netherlands, New Zealand, Norway, Spain, Switzerland, U.K.

12. Maritime transportation: coastal trade reserved to national flag carriers and restrictions on foreign ownership of such carriers or foreign-owned companies otherwise restricted: France, Germany, Greece, Italy, New Zealand, Portugal, Spain, U.S.

13. Maritime transportation: a percentage of imports is reserved to the national flag: Portugal, Spain, US.

14. Restrictions in ownership or registration of air transportation companies: Australia, Germany, Italy, Japan, Luxemboug, Netherlands, Spain, Switzerland, Turkey, U.K.

15. Air transportation: non-national carriers not permitted to carry passengers from one local point to another: all.

16. Air transportation: non-national airlines not permitted to establish their own ground handling facilities: France, Italy, Switzerland, Turkey.

III. ADDITIONAL REMARKS CONCERNING PUBLIC ORDER AND SECURITY AND INTERNATIONAL TRANSPORTATION ACTIVITIES

Public order and essential security interests

5.30. The CIME decided that restrictions based on public order and essential security interests should be reported in the interest of transparency and in order to ensure consistency in the understanding of what is covered by the provisions on public order and essential security interests (27). Public order generally relates to fundamental moral or legal precepts of a country and is evoked to frustrate the applicability of incompatible foreign laws or international agreements. The term "essential security interests" relates to matters affecting the defence and safety of the State.

5.31. In the present survey of measures relating to National Treatment, public order has not been specifically invoked as the basis for restrictive measures. Discriminatory measures in relation to foreign-controlled companies taken on the basis of essential security interests are found with some frequency among Member countries. Eleven countries (Australia, Austria, Denmark, Finland, France, Japan, Portugal, Spain, Sweden, U.K., U.S.) have indicated special restrictions on investment by established foreign-controlled enterprises in defence-related industries which could involve "essential security interests". In sectors in France relating directly or indirectly to national defence, limitations or guarantees relating to some foreign-controlled companies' investments in these sectors may be required. It seems likely that other countries do apply similar measures for the same reasons. Sectoral restrictions on investment activities by foreign-controlled enterprises are used relatively often in areas relating to public utilities and public services and not covered by public monopolies. All countries, for instance, have

46

reported such limitations with respect to air transportation. Two Delegations (Japan and the United States) in this context have specifically referred to considerations of "essential security interests". In regard to other sectors, in Japan, foreign-owned companies may be restricted in accordance with Japanese law, in atomic energy, arms manufacture, or narcotics, and in the Netherlands, the government reserves the right to prohibit foreign-owned companies from producing defence supplies in particular cases. In the United States the restrictions imposed on the activities of foreign-controlled enterprises in the area of communications (broadcasting, communications satellite corporation) are motivated by national security reasons.

5.32. One Delegation feels that an important motivation for exceptions to National Treatment is that of "essential national economic interests" which, like public order and essential security interests, is of a high order of importance, and should be reflected in the Declaration. The National Treatment instrument recognises that discriminatory measures may be taken for economic interests, cultural interests or other national geo-political interests but such measures clearly constitute exceptions to National Treatment. In contrast, measures taken on the basis of public order and essential security interests, traditionally recognised safeguard concepts of public international law, are not exceptions per se, but are to be reported in the interest of transparency. Here again, countries may vary in their perception of the need to discriminate against foreign-controlled enterprises but it is important that measures in fact taken for economic, cultural, or other interests be identified as such and not be shielded by a too extensive interpretation of public order and security interests. In the area of oil and gas exploration, for example, an exception reported by Canada is for important economic reasons, to increase domestic participation in this sector, while in Switzerland, restrictions on such activities with respect to foreign participation are based upon national security. In Japan, restrictions on oil production are based upon national resource and employment policy.

International transportation activities

5.33. The nature of numerous measures related to National Treatment in the air and maritime transportation sectors deserves special consideration. As indicated in Table 6 B, all OECD countries maintain exceptions in the air transportation area, whereby foreign-controlled carriers are generally not permitted to carry passengers from one local point to another. Ten countries restrict the ownership or registration of air transportation companies, thirteen countries restrict the percentage of foreign ownership of ships that are registered in the host country (national flag carriers) and most also maintain nationality requirements for company directors and managers, and eight countries reserve maritime coastal trade to national flag carriers.

5.34. In the maritime transportation sector, the main restrictions are of two types: i) limitations on foreign-ownership of ships if the ship wishes to be registered in the host country (fly the national flag) and ii) reservation of coastal trade to national flag carriers. At the international level, registration of ships is governed by the 1958 Convention on the High Sea (28). Article 5 of the 1958 Convention provides that "each State shall fix the conditions for the grant of its nationality to ships, for the registration of ships in its territory .... [and] there must exist a genuine link between the State and the ship; in particular, the State must effectively exercise its jurisdiction and control in administrative, technical and social matters over ships flying its flag". The National Treatment instrument recognises that foreign-controlled enterprises are to be treated consistent with international law. The practices of Member countries vary in establishing requirements for the registration of ships. Some countries have established ownership require-ments based on nationality that result in exceptions to National Treatment, while others have requirements that do not preclude foreign-controlled compa-nies from registering ships in a host country, usually through a locally-incorporated company. If limitations are placed on foreign ownership of national flag carriers, a shipping company whose foreign ownership exceeds the permissible limit will not be able to engage in coastal trade in a country that also limits coastal trade to national flag carriers. However, if foreign-controlled companies' ships may fly the national flag, such companies will not be restricted by coastal trade being limited to national flag carriers. In the air transportation sector, the Convention on International Civil Aviation of 1944 ("Chicago Convention") has established a practice whereby states negotiate bilaterally for the right of their airlines to ope-rate scheduled services on international routes. Certain bilateral agreements have allowed for foreign carriers to provide services between domestic cities; however, as indicated in paragraph 3.6 in the section on reciprocity, this does not imply that the measures concerned are not considered as exceptions to National Treatment.

5.35. As indicated in a clarification (29), measures of differential treat-ment between foreign-owned and locally-owned companies constitute exceptions to National Treatment when established foreign-controlled companies operating in any business sector cannot engage in particular activities. Accordingly, the restrictions on foreign ownership or nationality requirements indicated above are considered as exceptions or measures to be reported for transparency in relation to National Treatment, insofar as they apply to foreign-controlled companies established in the country concerned, whatever sector these may happen to be operating in. Thus for instance, according to the information reported in paragraph 5.33 above, all Member countries maintain exceptions in the air transportation sector. The issue has arisen whether service companies such as international transportation companies operating in a foreign country through representative offices, sales offices and agents, should be considered as established as is the case if they operate, for instance, through a subsi-diary. The Committee confirmed that measures restricting investment opera-tions of international transportation companies operating through branches, representative offices, sales offices and agents should be reported for pur-poses of transparency but would not constitute exceptions to National Treatment.

IV. THE RELATIVE IMPORTANCE OF MEASURES

5.36. In carrying out its work on clarifications of the scope of the National Treatment instrument and in relation to this new survey that increases the transparency of government measures bearing on National Treatment, the Committee considered that it would also be useful to provide an assessment of the relative importance of the impact on foreign investors of practice of the various measures related to National Treatment (30).

5.37.   The scope of the present assessment of the relative importance of measures related to National Treatment, both exceptions and others, must be considered in light of the nature of the available information on such measures. Although comparable data that could provide the basis for some quantitative analysis of the economic effects of measures is not available and would be costly to assemble, it is possible to identify certain aspects of the impact of measures that reflect on their relative importance.

5.38.   The relative importance of the impact on foreign investors of measures related to National Treatment will depend upon the extent of the effects of discriminatory measures on foreign-owned firms and will relate to such factors as the degree of the adverse impact on firms, the number of firms affected, the number and importance of economic sectors affected, and the number of Member countries that impose particular measures. The assessment below of the importance of reported measures considers these factors. The following paragraphs will discuss the economic effects of measures according to the categories in which they have been considered in this survey.

Categories of measures

5.39.   In its contributions on National Treatment, BIAC has stated that in terms of foregone revenue, <u>government procurement and public purchasing</u> may be the most significant area of discrimination against foreign-owned firms. Of course, the loss of a sale to a government agency may be quite apparent and the loss of sales revenue may be readily quantifiable, but other discriminatory measures may have more far reaching effects whose dimensions cannot be easily determined. As in the aids and subsidies category to be discussed below, large numbers of firms are affected by discrimination in public procurement, often in significant sectors of the economy such as telecommunications and other high technology sectors that service the military. Regarding the number of foreign firms affected by preferential government procurement, given the size of the public sector in general and of defence procurement in particular in Member countries, the number of foreign firms affected in this category of measures is undoubtedly large. BIAC has cited the computer industry as a leading example of where deliberate discriminatory government procurement measures have been used in recent years to develop locally-owned capability in large scale computers and also in micro-electronics and telecommunications. In this area, non-transparent practices and arcane procedures in awarding public contracts often makes competition difficult for foreign-owned firms. BIAC reports that sometimes discretion is exercised in publicising the availability of public contracts, that State and provincial governments are especially vulnerable to criticism in this area in the U.S., Australia and Canada, and that local governments also discriminate against foreign firms. BIAC, in 1982, also cited Canada, France, Japan, the United Kingdom and the United States as countries having had important discriminatory practices in this area. The distinction between restrictions relating to National Treatment and those relating to GATT obligations on procurement of imported products is often blurred in the view of enterprises. Under National Treatment, the concern is with procurement of goods produced locally by foreign-controlled firms, while GATT requirements relate to procurement of products made abroad (31).

5.40.   Fourteen Member countries have reported exceptions or other measures in this area. Measures reported by Member countries include: requirements for government employees to use national airlines or ferry services, reported by ten countries, whose impact is of moderate importance on foreign airlines and whose overall economic impact is considered to be low; the disqualification of foreign consulting firms from contracts for foreign aid projects, reported by three countries, whose overall impact is considered low; and preference for locally-owned firms and exclusion of foreign-controlled firms from some defence contracts, reported by four countries and whose impact is considered moderate.

5.41. Measures in the category of <u>government aids and subsidies</u> (32) have also been cited by BIAC as being among the most troublesome from the business point of view. During the present period of high unemployment and high unused capacity government aids and subsidies may well be growing although increasing budgetary constraints tend in some cases to moderate this trend. Furthermore, countries may not by design or by accident wish to favour systematically domestic firms. Within this category, financial relations between the State and publicly-owned firms in the competitive sector are also likely to be an area of interest all the more as such relations are not always very transparent. When the State is the sole or majority shareholder of either a public service or manufacturing enterprise, budgetary appropriations to such enterprises can amount to subsidies, as when such financial infusions compensate for operating losses rather than provide funding for expanded capacity. Foreign-owned firms competing with such State enterprises will not always have access to similar funding or to the same degree, as governments may in some cases behave in a different manner than private shareholders.

5.42. Transparency and predictability may also be lacking for aids and subsidies other than those granted to public-owned firms. Foreign-controlled firms, as well as others, want to know whether they will be subject to discriminatory measures, and, if so, on what basis. When some competitors receive government aids and subsidies, this is often an important factor that must be weighed in strategic planning. However, if the conditions of eligibility for government grants and the rates of award and their duration are unknown, business planning is made more difficult and less precise. From governments' point of view, however, it may often not be possible to commit itself well in advance on the eligibility and amount of grants that will assist planning in the affected sectors because such aids may depend upon budgetary and economic situations that may develop relatively quickly.

5.43. With regard to the impact on foreign-owned firms, aids and subsidies in the form of credits for new plant or equipment and grants for research and development are often significant and long lasting. Credits for new plants and equipment provided on a discriminatory basis are especially detrimental to the competitive position of foreign firms because of the increase in productive capacity of a competitor at substantially reduced cost. Grants for research and development on a discriminatory basis are also an irritant, especially in sectors where R & D is an important factor, such as in chemicals and microelectronics, or in low technology industries where R & D is often a residual expenditure, but can be important.

5.44. Twelve Member countries have notified the Organisation about some form of exception or other measures in the area of government aids and subsidies. Measures reported include: the provision of financial assistance and guarantees for the tourism industry, reported by six Member countries, whose overall impact is considered low; grants and priority for local oil and gas companies, reported by two countries, whose overall impact is considered moderate;

discrimination in the provision of loan guarantees and preferential credits, reported by two countries, applicable to many sectors including agriculture, and whose overall importance is considered moderate.

5.45. All Member countries maintain measures in the category of <u>investment by established foreign-controlled enterprises</u>. These generally take the form of limiting the expansion of multinational enterprises, either in particular sectors of economic activity, that are usually generally well known, such as domestic air transportation in most countries, or in ad hoc cases, as when mergers or acquisitions are subject to prior approval. When restrictions are imposed in ad hoc cases, the adverse effects of discrimination are not only immediate, but also there often is widespread publicity that may have the effect of discouraging potential foreign investors. Often the sectors in which restrictions apply to foreign firms are significant, such as maritime and air transportation, mining, oil production, banking, insurance and radio and TV broadcasting.

5.46. The restrictions on investments by foreign-owned firms will sometimes depend on the method of expansion, de novo or through a merger or acquisition, and where prior approval is required, the determination will sometimes depend upon the degree of foreign ownership of a particular sector. The lack of transparency and predictability of decisions on proposed mergers and acquisitions by foreign-controlled enterprises is also considered widespread. Often no firm criteria can be made available because an acquisition by an established foreign-controlled enterprise will be permitted only if there are no suitable or willing domestic firms to make the acquisition. This is especially the case when the target company's prospects for continued viability are doubtful. Sometimes the stated criterion is the "public interest" which is too vague to be helpful as a guide to predictability. In view of the number of Member countries that impose exceptions in this category and the importance of the sectors of the economy from which foreign-controlled enterprises are excluded, this category is one of the most important. Measures reported that occur with some frequency are: prior approval procedures for: expansion of investments in any field (two countries), expansion of activities in non-related areas (six countries), takeover bids, for certain sectors or in EEC countries by non-EEC companies (nine countries), whose impact on companies and overall impact is considered moderate to high; authorisation required and/or ownership restrictions on investments in the mining and natural resources sectors, reported by eight countries whose overall impact is considered moderate; and restrictions on domestic airline traffic and maritime coastal trade, reported by all countries for airlines and half the countries for shipping, whose impact on transportation companies is high, but whose overall impact is moderate to low.

5.47. The category of exceptions relating to <u>access to local bank credit and the capital market</u> has been relatively unimportant for non-financial multinational enterprises, according to information supplied by BIAC. Only six Member countries have notified such restrictions, which generally require authorisation for foreign firms to borrow and may impose conditions on such borrowing, such as a limit in relation to equity capital or foreign financing. Thus, the cost of some amount of financing is at issue, rather than engaging in activities or competing for significant sales, as in other categories. The rules regarding authorisations are also fairly well known in this category, which is probably another reason why exceptions in this area are less troublesome.

5.48. In regard to tax measures several of the matters which have been cited as troublesome for multinational enterprises -- imputation systems, higher tax rates for branches than for subsidiaries, dividend taxes, consolidation rules and unitary systems -- relate to difficulties created by the fact of the relationship of non-resident taxpayers to a company in a foreign country rather than by differential treatment between resident locally-owned and resident foreign-owned firms, so that in such cases the concept of National Treatment is not directly in question. In assessing the relative importance of exceptions to National Treatment therefore, the tax measures cited above have not been included as they do not fall properly under the National Treatment instrument. Other tax measures that may properly relate to National Treatment are found only infrequently the OECD countries and seem not to have a major importance.

Comparative assessment

5.49. Considering the relative importance of reported measures related to National Treatment as a whole, certain generalisations are apparent. In regard to the manner of application of exceptions, the number of measures applied automatically and those applied on a discretionary basis seem to be about evenly divided. The application of measures also appears to be preponderantly sector-specific rather than generally applicable to all business activities. The sectors most affected are oil exploration and mining, banking, insurance, and air and maritime transportation. Measures also generally have the effect of limiting the scope of foreign-owned companies' activities in a field rather than prohibiting their engaging in a field. Thus, for example, in the area of government aids and subsidies, the discrimination against foreign companies in granting credits and in government procurement, the differential treatment of domestic firms does not prevent the continuing activities of foreign companies, but limits their sales and development.

5.50. If one were to rank the importance of the five categories of measures, the two least important are clearly tax obligations and access to local bank credit and the capital markets. Of the three more important categories, on the basis of reported measures, that of official aids and subsidies appears somewhat less important than government procurement because discriminatory official aids appear less widespread among Member countries than discriminatory procurement. Restrictions in the area of investments by established foreign-controlled enterprises appear to be the most widespread. Furthermore, measures in this category may permanently or severely limit the ability of foreign firms to engage in activities in a wide range of sectors, whereas measures in the other two important categories generally limit some aspect of business activities, perhaps at only one point in time, such as the inability to compete for a particular government contract or the failure to receive some grant for research and development. Restrictions imposed on foreign-controlled firms in important sectors of activity, such as banking, oil production and mining, or on particular investment opportunities, for instance when authorisation is denied for takeover bids, will also be detrimental to the investment climate in the countries that have discriminatory measures in relation to investment by established foreign-controlled companies.

5.51. In considering the relative importance of measures related to National Treatment in the 1983 survey, the trend in measures taken since the last survey in 1978 should also be considered. As indicated in paragraph 5.4 above, while the present survey contains a listing of considerably more

measures than the last survey, this results essentially from a better understanding of the scope of the instrument, from better sources of information
and from the recent agreement that a number of additional measures, other than
exceptions to National Treatment, are to be reported, rather than from an increase in significant new discriminatory practices.

5.52. Of new measures reported since 1978, the most significant are those by
Canada related to the oil and gas industry. Under the Petroleum Incentive
Programme Act of 1982, certain payments for costs of oil and gas exploration
are made on a graduated basis related to the level of Canadian equity participation and under the Canada Oil and Gas Act of 1982, exploration agreements
may require that Canadian equity participation and production licenses are
issued to (at least 50 per cent) Canadian-owned enterprises. Portugal introduced a law in 1982 whereby 25 per cent foreign-owned companies must receive
approval to acquire more than 50 per cent of another company in Portugal.
Removal of significant restrictions on foreign-controlled enterprises were
taken by the United Kingdom in government procurement of computers and in
access to foreign borrowing by established foreign-controlled enterprises.

1. The texts of the latter two instruments and the related OECD Council Decisions are included in Annex I. A comprehensive OECD publication on the Guidelines is forthcoming.

2. The various instruments of international co-operation involved embody different types of obligations on the part of Member States and represent various commitments of Member countries and governments. Concerning such differences, the reader should consult, inter alia, the Convention of the Organisation for Economic Co-operation and Development.

3. OECD's principle of National Treatment is somewhat different than the trade concept contained in the General Agreement on Tariffs and Trade (GATT) of national treatment for products of foreign origin, although both concepts have as their objective the promotion of competition in trade and investment free of discriminatory government actions because of foreign origin or ownership. Under Article III of the GATT, imported products of a party to the GATT shall be accorded treatment no less favourable than that accorded to like products of national origin in respect of all requirements affecting their sale or use. Thus the GATT principle of National Treatment refers to non-discrimination between products of local and foreign origin, while the OECD principle of National Treatment refers to non-discrimination between domestic and foreign-owned or -controlled enterprises operating in the country in question.

4. International Investment and Multinational Enterprises: The 1979 Review Report, OECD, 1979. International Investment and Multinational Enterprises: The Mid-Term Report, OECD, 1982. International Investment and Multinational Enterprises: The 1984 Review Report, OECD, 1984.

5. See also paragraph 4.5 for a discussion of the distinction between "operating in their territory" and "establishment", a distinction which is relevant for the category of measures relating to investments by established foreign-controlled companies in a given country.

6. The OECD Code of Liberalisation of Capital Movements, OECD, 1982.

7. Model Double Taxation Convention on Income and on Capital, OECD, 1977.

8. As in recent tax treaties such as those concluded by the U.K. and France, where the benefit of the tax credit is extended to foreign portfolio shareholders and, in the case of the UK, half of the credit is granted to foreign direct shareholders.

9. Transfer Pricing and Multinational Enterprises, OECD, Paris, 1979; paragraphs 170-173.

10. See International Investment and Multinational Enterprises: The Responsibility of Parent Companies for their Subsidiaries, OECD, 1980; paragraphs 41-46.

11. The use of unitary tax systems or so-called global methods of profit allocation between affiliated entities has been rejected in the above-mentioned Report on Transfer Pricing and Multinational Enterprises as arbitrary and particularly burdensome for the operation of multi-national enterprises. (See paragraph 14 of the Report).

12. National Treatment for Foreign-Controlled Enterprises Established in OECD Countries, OECD, 1978.

13. National Treatment: A Major International Investment Issue of the 1980s, BIAC Committee on International Investment and Multinational Enterprises, 1982.

14. See Mid-Term Report, Annex V, paragraph 30.

15. Mid-Term Report, paragraph 34.

16. 1979 Review Report, paragraphs 94 and 110.

17. Mid-Term Report, Annex V, paragraph 8.

18. Mid-Term Report, Annex V, paragraph 5.

19. 1979 Review Report, paragraph 114.

20. Second Revised Decision of the Council on National Treatment, paragraph 3.

21. There is in this respect one difference with the 1978 survey on National Treatment. There, an additional category, of "internal regula-tions and practices" was considered. Since measures that were grouped in this category generally relate to a governmental activity like aids and subsidies or taxation or to an enterprise activity like a new investment, such measures should usually not be considered separately from the activity in question in which differential treatment is exer-cised. They were so considered in 1978 only because of insufficient transparency of government measures and lack of clarity as to the scope of the instrument. Progress on these two subjects has allowed the Committee to consider these measures under the main categories and eliminate the "internal regulations and practices" category. The Committee reaffirmed the importance of transparency in this area and encouraged all Member countries to notify such measures.

22. Mid-Term Report, Annex V, paragraphs 15-25.

23. Article 24, paragraph 6 of the Model Convention states that "Enter-prises of a Contracting State, the capital of which is wholly or partly owned or controlled, directly or indirectly, by one or more residents of the other Contracting State, shall not be subjected in the first-mentioned State to any taxation or any requirement connected therewith which is other or more burdensome than the taxation and connected

requirements to which other similar enterprises of the first-mentioned State are or may be subjected". Paragraph 4 of Article 24 also specifically refers to branches of enterprises as benefitting from non-discrimination. The main difference between the two instruments relevant here is the fact that the National Treatment Instrument refers only to the notion of control, while Article 24 of the Model Convention refers to total or partial ownership and control.

24. It may be useful to recall the forms under which investments by established foreign companies are generally made:

-- Growth of the foreign-controlled enterprise;

    i) Through reinvested profits and local borrowing;
    ii) With injection of fresh foreign capital.

-- Extension (by whatever techniques) in the same line of business or related area;

-- Creation of new activities (by fully-owned enterprises or joint ventures) in different lines of business;

-- Participation in or takeover of existing national enterprises.

25. Of countries that maintain controls on new inward direct investment, some also retain controls on investments by established foreign-controlled enterprises, while others do not. For instance, in the area of access to local sources of financing for inward direct investment, a survey of Member countries showed that eight countries that restricted local financing of new inward direct investments by non-resident enterprises maintained no special financing restrictions for established foreign-controlled enterprises.

26. Authorisation or notification procedures, where authorisation may be rejected only if the operation is not in fact in conformity with what is stated by the investor, or for public order and essential security interests, or for other reasons that fall outside the scope of the National Treatment Instrument are not considered here.

27. See chapter III for further clarifications of these terms.

28. This Convention has been amplified by the recently signed Law of the Sea Convention that will supercede the 1958 Convention if ratified by the requisite number of countries.

29. See section 3.6 above.

30. The Mid-Term Report on the 1976 Declarations and Decisions, OECD, 1982, paragraphs 38 et seq., recognised that an assessment of the relative importance of exceptions to National Treatment would be an objective of the work of the Committee.

31. See Mid-Term Report, Annex V e).

32. Fiscal aids and subsidies are considered in this category of measures rather than in the category of tax obligations.

Annex I

MEMBER COUNTRY MEASURES RELATED TO NATIONAL TREATMENT

NOTES ON ANNEX I

1.   The lists of measures for each Member country are arranged as follows:

a) Measures that constitute exceptions to National Treatment, followed by;

b) Measures (on page(s) labelled "Transparency" at the top) which are reported in the interest of transparency. These measures are generally those based on essential security interests or applied only to branches of foreign-controlled companies (non-residents) in host countries. The description of the measure and the motivation often explain why the measure has been reported.

2.   Where a measure is described generally (such as "financial assistance and guarantees" for the tourism sector for several countries) it is to be presumed that the measure represents more favourable treatment for locally-owned enterprises as compared to foreign-owned enterprises.

Category	Measure	Sector	Authority/ Administration	Automatic/ Discretionary	Motivation/ Results	Other Information
Official Aids and Subsidies	Branches not eligible for research and development incentives.	All				
Access to Financing	None.					
Tax Obligations	None.					
Government Procurement	Requirements for government employees to use national airlines/ferry services.	Tourism				
Government Procurement	The Middle East Technical Support Facility (METSF) is a programme to provide advice on a government to government basis to Middle East Countries, and is open only to locally-owned firms. The programme is scheduled to expire in 1983/84. The Minister for Trade has proposed its continuation; whether it will be in operation in 1984/85 is a matter for government consideration.	Consultancy	Commonwealth Department of Trade	Automatic	To ensure that Australian firms have the opportunity of participation in development projects in the Middle-East/demonstrated effectiveness.	Duration: scheduled to expire in 1983/84, under review. 1982/83 budget: A\$ 300 000
Government Procurement	Under the Consulting Services Feasibility Study Fund (CSFSF) programme, the government commissions feasibility studies for projects in developing countries. Only locally-owned firms are eligible.	Consultancy	Commonwealth Department of Trade	Automatic	To develop the export of Australian expertise.	Duration: indefinite 1982/83 budget: A\$ 450 000
Investments by Established Companies	Authorisation is required for established foreign-controlled firms: to diversify their activities into non-related areas: to acquire a controlling interest in an existing enterprise in Australia through other arrangements falling within the scope of the foreign takeovers act 1975: and to undertake new development projects in the areas of real estate, mining, minerals processing, agriculture, pastoral activities, forestry and fishing.	All; certain sectors	Treasurer/ Foreign Investment Review Board	Discretionary	To ensure investments harmonize with Australian interests. The measures listed as affecting investment by established companies arise from the provisions of the foreign takeovers act, legislation concerning	Duration: indefinite

Category	Measure	Sector	Authority/ Administration	Automatic/ Discretionary	Motivation/ Results	Other Information
					specific sectors and other elements of foreign investment policy in relation to the establishment of new activities in Australia by foreign interests. Foreign investment policy has been essentially directed to the right of establishment.	
Investments by Established Companies	Investment by foreign-controlled enterprises is restricted in the service sector of the economy under the following legislation: The Banking Act 1959. It had been the policy of all governments since the Banking Act was first enacted in 1945 not to grant foreign interests authority to carry on banking business in Australia or to allow them to acquire interests, other than of a small portfolio nature, in existing Australian banks. On 13 January 1983 the then Treasurer announced the Government's decision, in principle to allow for the initial entry of around ten banks with foreign shareholdings; into the Australian Banking System. On 29 May the new Government announced that it commissioned the Australian Financial System Group (the Martin Group) to prepare a report on the structure of the financial system, including the question of foreign bank entry. The Group's terms of reference stated that the report should have regard to the recommendations of the earlier committee of inquiry into the Australian financial system and take into account the Government's economic and social objectives as well as the	Banking	Treasurer/ Foreign Investment Review Board			

AUSTRALIA

Category	Measure	Sector	Authority/ Administration	Automatic/ Discretionary	Motivation/ Results	Other Information
	need to improve the efficiency of the financial system. The report was completed towards the end of 1983, and its recommendations are currently subject to the Government's consideration.					
Investments by Established Companies	To engage in new non-bank financial services or establish a new insurance company, a foreign-owned firm must show substantial economic benefits or, where economic benefits are small, the venture must involve an effective partnership with local interests in the ownership and control of the company concerned. It has been the policy of successive Australian Governments since 1945 not to grant foreign interests authority to carry on banking business in Australia.	Financial services and insurance companies	Treasurer/ Foreign Investment Review Board	Discretionary		
Investments by Established Companies	Foreign investment in radio and television is governed by the Broadcasting and Television Act 1942. The Act provides that a "foreign person", as defined by that Act, may not hold or control, directly or indirectly, more than 15 per cent of the issued capital or voting rights in a licensee company, and that two or more "foreign persons" may not hold or control in aggregate more than 20 per cent of the issued capital or voting rights in a licensee company.	Broadcasting and television	Broadcasting Tribunal/ Broadcasting and Television Act	Automatic		
Investments by Estalished Companies	Participation by foreign interests in mass circulation newspapers is restricted and all investments, other than portfolio investments that do not fall within the scope of the foreign takeovers act, are subject to case-by-case assessment.	Newspaper publishing	Treasurer/ Foreign Investment Review Board	Discretionary		
Investments by Established Companies	Non-national airlines are not permitted to carry passengers from one national point to another.	Air transportation	Department of Transport			

60

AUSTRALIA

Category	Measure	Sector	Authority/ Administration	Automatic/ Discretionary	Motivation/ Results	Other Information
Investments by Established Companies	Foreign shareholding in casinos in the State of Tasmania is limited to 38 per cent.	Casinos	Tasmanian Government			
Investments by Established Companies	Foreign investment in domestic airlines is restricted and all investments in civil aviation, other than portfolio investments that do not fall within the scope of the foreign takeovers act, are subject to case-by-case assessment. Unless the Secretary to the Department of Transport other wise directs, a licence or certificate required under the air navigation regulations shall not be issued to a person who is not a British subject ordinarily resident in Australia or a corporation substantially owned and effectively controlled by British subjects ordinarily resident in Australia. Certificates and licences referred to include Certificates of Approval in relation to manufacture, distribution and maintenance of aircraft and aircraft components and materials, and Aerial Work Charter and Airline Licences for the operations of air services.	Aircraft manufacture Air transportation	Treasurer/ Foreign Investment Review Board	Discretionary		
Investments by Established Companies	There is control of transfers of pastoral leases in Western Australia with a view to ensuring that at least 50 per cent Australian equity is maintained. Under the provisions of both Acts a pastoral lease cannot be transferred without the written consent of the Minister for Lands and Surveys or of an officer authorised in that behalf by the Governor. The Minister's discretion is absolute.	Agriculture (Western Australia)	Western Australian Government

The Land Act 1933 and Transfer of Land Act 1893 | Discretionary | The desirability of land in Western Australia remaining in the hands of domiciled Western Australians or Australians. To ensure that Australian equity in pastoral leases is maintained at not less than 50 per cent. | Indefinite duration |

AUSTRALIA: TRANSPARENCY

Category	Measure	Sector	Authority/ Administration	Automatic/ Discretionary	Motivation/ Results	Other Information
Official Aids and Subsidies	Financial assistance and tax incentives may be granted for the production and distribution of films with significant Australian content. Factors to consider include the residence of the production company.	Film production	Australian Film Commission Minister for Home Affairs and Environment	Discretionary	To encourage the development of an economically viable Australian film production industry	
Tax Obligations	The special deductions available in respect of capital expenditure on the production of qualifying Australian films are allowable only where the expenditure is made by an Australian resident.	Films	Minister for Home Affairs and Environment			
Tax Obligations	A corporate income tax, known as a "Branch Profits Tax" is imposed upon income of a non-resident company deriving income directly from operations in Australia. The tax is in addition to any other income tax payable by the company.	All		Automatic		
Investments by Established Companies	Specific guidelines for Australian participation have applied in respect of new natural resource projects and, in certain circumstances, in relation to new investments in the finance and insurance and real estate sectors. In other sectors Australian participation has been sought subject to the particular commercial and other circumstances of each case. Proposals falling within the scope of the Foreign Takeovers Act are required to demonstrate sufficient benefits to offset losses of Australian ownership and control. These provisions have applied to all foreign interests establishing in Australia whether or not they have previously invested in Australia.	Natural resources, finance, insurance, real estate	Treasurer/ Foreign Investment Review Board			

Category	Measure	Sector	Authority/ Administration	Automatic/ Discretionary	Motivation/ Results	Other Information
Investments by Established Companies	The Government may, as appropriate, allow proposals that do not fully comply with the requirements of foreign investment policy to proceed subject to the parties agreeing to certain conditions. This allows some flexibility to foreign interests in meeting the requirements of policy. Such conditions may, for example, allow a period of time for foreign interests to meet equity requirements or other elements of policy subject to normal commercial circumstances. Other types of conditions may require the parties to proposals to consult with other Federal, State or local government authorities on such matters as taxation, the environment and zoning regulations. In respect of real estate acquisitions, a common condition of approval is to require the parties to re-sell property to Australians or other eligible interests once the purpose for its acquisition no longer exists. As appropriate, the Government requires foreign interests to report regularly on progress made in fulfilling such conditions.	All	Treasurer/ Foreign Investment Review Board			

AUSTRIA

Category	Measure	Sector	Authority/ Administration	Automatic/ Discretionary	Motivation/ Results	Other Information
Official Aids and Subsidies	State-owned oil companies may be given preferential prices for supplies and use of crude oil.	Oil Industry				
Official Aids and Subsidies	Provision of financial assistance.	Tourism				
Tax Obligations	None.					
Access to Financing	None.					
Government Procurement	Preference for domestic suppliers.	Defence				
Investments by Established Companies	Foreign-controlled companies must apply for authorisation before undertaking a project.	All				
Investments by Established Companies	Foreign-controlled companies wishing to undertake investments in the form of loans will be granted authorisations only if the project serves to increase productive capacity.	All		Discretionary		
Investments by Established Companies	A newly established foreign-owned bank is not permitted to take savings deposits (such restriction is removed later). Foreign-owned banks in Austria are not permitted to manage or participate in the underwriting of securities issues.	Banking				
Investments by Established Companies	Provincial regulations regarding the acquisition of real estate by established foreign-controlled companies.	Real estate				
Investments by Established Companies	Non-national airlines are not permitted to carry passengers from one national point to another.	Air Transportation				
Investments by Established Companies	Ships registered in Austria must be 75 per cent locally owned.	Maritime transportation				

AUSTRIA: TRANSPARENCY

Category	Measure	Sector	Authority/ Administration	Automatic/ Administration	Motivation/ Results	Other Information
Investments by Established Companies	Acquisition of real estate must be approved by the Real Estate Commission of provincial and municipal administrations.	Real estate				

BELGIUM

Category	Measure	Sector	Authority/ Administration	Automatic/ Discretionary	Motivation/ Results	Other Information
Official Aids and Subsidies	None.					
Tax Obligations	None.					
Access to Financing	None.					
Government Procurement	None.					
Investments by Established Companies	Direct or indirect acquisitions by non-EEC companies of Belgian companies is subject to authorisation for any takeover bid for public companies.	All	Minister of Finance	Discretionary	The purpose is to consider the compatability of the proposed acquisition with the state of the local financial market.	

BELGIUM: TRANSPARENCY

Category	Measure	Sector	Authority/ Administration	Automatic/ Discretionary	Motivation/ Results	Other Information
Tax Obligations	Branches in Belgium of foreign companies are subject to a higher rate of corporate income taxes than companies incorporated in Belgium (1982 54 per cent versus 48 per cent 1983: 50 per cent versus 45 per cent), in the absence of a double taxation treaty that generally eliminates this tax-rate difference.	All		Automatic		
Tax Obligations	Withholding taxes on dividends received by branches of foreign companies in Belgium is not credited towards income tax payable in Belgium by such branches, whereas such dividend withholding taxes are credited against taxes owed by locally-incorporated companies that receive such dividends.	All		Automatic	This measure results from an attempt at tax neutrality, regardless of the form of corporate structure of an enterprise in Belgium since a subsidiary in Belgium of a foreign company pays withholding tax on dividends remitted to the foreign parent company.	
Investments by Established Companies	Branches of foreign owned enterprises must receive prior authorisation to act as lead managers of underwritings of securities issued in local currency on the local capital market.	Investment Banking				According to the Belgian authorities, this authorisation is granted routinely.
Investments by Established Companies	Non-national carriers are not permitted to carry passengers from one national point to another.	Air transportation			Public Monopoly	

67

CANADA

Category	Measure	Sector	Authority/ Administration	Automatic/ Discretionary	Motivation/ Results	Other Information
Official Aids and Subsidies	The Petroleum Incentives Programme provides a system of direct grants to oil and gas exploration companies. In the Canada lands, all companies, both domestic and foreign, receive a grant of 25 per cent of their eligible exploration expenses. Higher level grants may be made to Canadian-controlled companies that have at least 50 per cent Canadian beneficial ownership. Incentive grants for Canadian-controlled and largely Canadian-owned companies are also available for exploration in the provincial lands, as are modest grants for development work in all areas. By agreement between the concerned governments, incentive payments for activities within the Province of Alberta are funded and administered by that Province.	Oil Industry			In 1980 foreign control of Canada's oil and gas production revenues was at a level of 77.7 per cent and foreign ownership of those revenues was at 72.0 per cent. In recognition of this, and of the fact that a high proportion of the exploration permits in the Canada lands (offshore and frontier lands not forming part of any province of Canada) was held by foreign-controlled firms, the government enacted legislation during 1980-82 to provide for a greater participation by Canadians in the general exploration and development of oil and gas, and also to accelerate the pace of activity in the geologically promising Canada lands, as a means of adding to Canada's oil and gas reserves.	
Official Aids and Subsidies	Under the Agricultural Development Act, to be eligible for a loan or loan guarantee by the Alberta Agricultural Development Corporation, an applicant must be a Canadian resident. A corporation is eligible for a loan provided that it is a resident of Alberta; that it is incorporated in Canada; and that non-resident ownership and control does not exceed 20 per cent of the issued and outstanding shares. The same general condition applies to a partnership with non-resident owners.	Agriculture (Alberta Province)	Agricultural Development Act		To provide encouragement to the Canadian owned sector in the form of assistance provided by tax payers.	
Official Aids and Subsidies	Regulations provide for grants to persons who intend to do exploratory work in Northern Canada. Such persons must in general be either Canadian citizens or a Canadian corporation whose shares are either owned at least 50 per cent by Canadians or listed on a Canadian stock exchange.	Mineral exploration		Automatic	To encourage Canadian participation in Northern mineral development and Canadian equity participation in foreign-owned mineral companies.	

68

Category	Measure	Sector	Authority/Administration	Automatic/Discretionary	Motivation/Results	Other Information
Official Aids and Subsidies	The Western Grain Stabilization Act provides for stabilization payments to grain producers. To be eligible for such payments the producer must be a) a Canadian citizen or a landed immigrant; or b) a corporation with more than 50 per cent of its shares owned by the Canadian citizens or landed immigrants.	Grain production	Western Grain Stabilization Act	Automatic	To encourage Canadian ownership of the grain industry	
Official Aids and Subsidies	In providing loans or other assistance to commercial enterprises in Alberta, the Alberta Opportunity Company is required to give priority to those enterprises owned and operated by Canadian citizens residing in the Province.	Commerce (Alberta Province)	Alberta Opportunity Fund Act		To provide special encouragement to the Canadian owned sector in the form of assistance provided by taxpayers.	
Official Aids and Subsidies	Regulations made under the Act stipulate that the Quebec Government may grant subsidies for the publication and distribution of books only to companies or corporations that, inter alia, are 50 per cent owned (with voting rights) by Canadian citizens or corporations domiciled in Quebec.	Publishing (Quebec Province)	Booksellers Accreditation Act		To provide special encouragement to the Canadian owned sector in the form of assistance provided by taxpayers.	
Official Aids and Subsidies	To be considered eligible for financial assistance, a farmer must be a Canadian citizen or a landed immigrant residing in Saskatchewan. The same condition holds for each member in respect of a farming partnership or co-operative farming association, and for each shareholder in respect of a farming corporation.	Agriculture (Saskatchewan Province)	Agricultural Incentives Act		To provide special encouragement to the Canadian owned sector in the form of assistance provided by taxpayers.	
Tax Obligations	Provincial: a) Ontario: The Land Transfer Tax on acquisitions of land and shares in farming or land corporations by non-residents is higher than the tax applicable to residents. A "non-resident" corporation is defined in the context of	Recreation and agricultural land	Land Transfer Tax Act/Ministry of Revenue of Ontario	Automatic	To encourage Canadian ownership of urban land	

CANADA

Category	Measure	Sector	Authority/ Administration	Automatic/ Discretionary	Motivation/ Results	Other Information
	ownership of its shareholdings or occupancy of directors' positions by non-resident individuals. A deferral or remission may be made in defined circumstances.					
Tax Obligations	b) Quebec: Land Transfer Duties Act. Under this Act a duty is levied on the transfer of land to "non-resident persons". In addition, when control of an existing corporation owning principally land is acquired by "non-resident persons", either from a resident or another non-resident, such corporation becomes liable for land transfer duties. A corporation is non-resident when more than 50 per cent of its voting capital stock or more than 50 per cent of its directors are non-resident individuals. Exemptions from duties can be made in several defined circumstances.	All	Land Transfer Duties Act/ Ministry of Revenue of Quebec	Automatic	To encourage Canadian ownership of Quebec land.	
Government	Government employees urged to use national airlines/ferry services.	Tourism				
Government Procurement	Under administrative guidelines, Ontario government advertising contracts are only to be awarded to wholly-owned Canadian companies or organisations. Companies are interpreted as those where shares are 100 per cent owned by Canadian citizens and/or wholly-owned Canadian companies and whose directors are all Canadian citizens.	Advertising (Ontario Province)			To provide special encouragement to the Canadian owned sector in the form of assistance provided by taxpayers.	
Investments by Established Companies	Foreign Investment Review Act. The Foreign Investment Review Act gives the Government authority to review investment proposals by non-eligible persons to determine whether or not they are likely to be of "significant benefit" to Canada.	All except banking	Foreign Investment Review Agency (FIRA)	Discretionary	(see measure)	

Category	Measure	Sector	Authority/Administration	Automatic/Discretionary	Motivation/Results	Other Information
	The Act applies in the establishment of new business, the acquisition of a Canadian business enterprise by foreign-controlled Canadian companies, and the expansion by such companies into unrelated business activities. Generally speaking a non-eligible person is a foreign individual; a government or an agency of a foreign government; or a corporation that is controlled by one or more non-eligible persons.					
Investments by Established Companies	Foreign ownership in Canadian-controlled and federally incorporated life insurance companies, trust companies, loan companies and investment companies is generally limited to 25 per cent of the capital stock, with no single foreign shareholder owning more than 10 per cent. Some provinces have adopted similar restrictions for companies incorporated under their jurisdiction.	Insurance Companies, Trust Companies, Finance Companies	Canadian and British Insurance Companies Act. Trust Companies Act. Loan Companies Act. Investment Companies Act.			Note: This restriction applies to companies incorporated in Canada owned by foreign corporations. In the case of a Canadian company owned directly by individuals, restrictions apply to non-resident owners rather than to non-Canadian nationals.
Investments by Established Companies	Section 10 of the Canada Oil and Gas Act and more specifically paragraph 10(2)(d) of the Act provides that the minister may enter into an exploration agreement in respect of Canada lands with a party and that the agreement may provide for any relevant matter including, inter alia, equity participation by Canadians.

Subsection 19(1) of the Act provides that no production license shall be issued unless the beneficial owner of the license: | Oil and Gas Production | Canada Oil and Gas Act | | The specific reason for this exception is rooted in the rationale of the Canadian National Energy Programme which, is mainly designed to increase energy security in and Canadian participation in the oil and gas sector. Specifically this exception aims at maximizing the opportunities for Canadian-controlled firms to engage in oil and gas exploration and production on Canada lands. | |

CANADA

Category	Measure	Sector	Authority/Administration	Automatic/Discretionary	Motivation/Results	Other Information
	1) If an individual, would be a Canadian citizen ordinarily resident in Canada or a permanent resident within the meaning of the Immigration Act, 1976, other than one who has been ordinarily resident in Canada for more than one year after the time at which he first became eligible to apply for Canadian citizenship;					
	2) If a corporation, would be incorporated in Canada and have a Canadian ownership rate of not less than 50 per cent; or					
	3) If two or more individuals or corporations or individuals and corporations would be comprised of individuals referred to in paragraph 1) or corporations incorporated in Canada or both and would have a Canadian ownership rate of not less than 50 per cent.					
Investments by Established Companies	Companies engaged in uranium production must undertake to fulfil the following three objectives: to achieve 67 per cent Canadian ownership; or a minimum of 50 per cent Canadian ownership combined with Canadian control; or a minimum of 50 per cent Canadian ownership combined with significant benefit to Canada. There are no ownership requirements concerning uranium exploration.	Uranium production	Ministry of Energy Mines and Resources		To maintain Canadian ownership and significant benefit to Canada	Duration indefinite
Investments by Established Companies	A licence to operate a broadcasting station, or permission to operate a network of broadcasting stations, can only be granted to a Canadian citizen or to a Canadian corporation of which four-fifths of the shares are owned either by Canadian-controlled corporations. An exception may be allowed in the case of an application for the	Broadcasting	Broadcasting Act Directives		The measure is designed to maintain Canadian control of broadcasting.	

Category	Measure	Sector	Authority/ Administration	Automatic/ Discretionary	Motivation/ Results	Other Information
	renewal of a broadcasting licence outstanding on 1st April 1968, providing the Commission is satisfied that granting a renewal would not run contrary to public interest and providing the Governor in Council, by order, approves such a renewal.					
Investments by Established Companies	Mining leases in the North-West Territories can only be granted to a Canadian citizen, or to a corporation incorporated in Canada the shares of which are either 50 per cent beneficially-owned by Canadian citizens or listed on a recognised Canadian stock exchange, and Canadians will have an opportunity of participating in the financial and ownership of the corporation.	Mining (North-West Territories)				
Investments by Established Companies	A number of provinces (Manitoba, Alberta, British Columbia) maintain laws or regulations requiring owners of land, normally agricultural or recreational, to be Canadian citizens or Canadian controlled corporations. Nova Scotia has a disclosure requirement for non-resident holdings of land sector.	Land	Public Lands Act Regulations	Automatic	To ensure Canadian ownership of agricultural and recreational land	Indefinite duration
Investments by Established Companies	A corporation can not carry on business in Ontario as a distributor if non-residents hold or control more than 25 per cent of the shares; or a single non-resident holds or controls more than 10 per cent of the shares; or if the corporation is incorporated outside Canada.	Periodical Distribution (Ontario Province)	Paperback and Periodicals Distributions Act of Ontario		Cultural	
Investments by Established Companies	Non-national airlines are not permitted to carry passengers from one national point to another.	Air transportation			Bilateral air agreements	

CANADA: TRANSPARENCY

Category	Measure	Sector	Authority/ Administration	Automatic/ Discretionary	Motivation/ Results	Other Information
Tax Obligations	Federal corporations organised abroad and not resident in Canada (and partnerships with non-resident partners) not eligible for tax-free roll-overs of assets and corporations cannot qualify for certain special status corporations like Investment Corporations.	All	Income Tax Act			
Tax Obligations	Small Canadian-controlled private corporations are accorded lower income tax rates on active business income derived from activities carried on in Canada.	All	Income Tax Act		The measure provides special incentives for Canadian-controlled small businesses so as to permit them to become established, to grow and to eventually turn into large competitive corporations.	
Investments by Established Companies	Regulations under the Ontario Securities Act provide for registration, or a renewal of registration, if the applicant is a resident and if the total number of shares held or controlled by non-residents as a group does not exceed 25 per cent of the outstanding shares; if no single non-resident, in conjunction with his associates, holds or controls more than 10 per cent of the outstanding shares; and where the applicant is a company, it is incorporated in Canada. The OSC may conditionally grant registration in spite of the restrictions if, in its opinion, such action is not detrimental to the public interest. Some other provinces, such as Saskatchewan, have similar rules.	Securities Brokerage (Provinces)	Ontario Securities Act; Discretionary Regulations	Discretionary		
Investments by Established Companies	Until a recent government review, domestic assets for all foreign bank subsidiaries could not exceed 8 per cent of the total domestic assets of all banks in Canada. Following this review, the ceiling has now been raised to 16 per cent. This measure	Banking	Bank Act/ Inspector General of Banks	Automatic	To allow an orderly entry of foreign banks in the Canadian banking market while preserving Canadian control	

DENMARK: TRANSPARENCY

Category	Measure	Sector	Authority/ Administration	Automatic/ Discretionary	Motivation/ Results	Other Information
Investments by Established Companies	The production of war material is reserved for domestic corporations owned by nationals.	War material		Automatic	National defence	

Category	Measure	Sector	Authority/ Administration	Automatic/ Discretionary	Motivation/ Results	Other Information
Official Aids and Subsidies	Provision of financial assistance and guarantees.	Tourism	The Finnish Tourist Board, The Regional Development Fund, Ministry of Trade and Industry			
Access to Financing	None.					
Tax Obligations	Foreign-owned companies without limited liability may have debt considered as equity for purposes of the capital tax.	All	National Board of Taxation	Discretionary	Prevention of tax evasion	Companies with limited liability are exempt from the capital tax.
Government Procurement	None					
Investments by Established Companies	Foreign-controlled resident enterprises must seek the prior authorisation of the government to establish a company.	All	Ministry of Trade and Industry	Automatic		According to the Finnish authorities these measures concern cases where the new company would operate outside the resident enterprise's original permit.
Investments by Established Companies	For foreign ownership of a Finnish company to exceed 20 per cent, authorisations are required.	All	Ministry of Trade and Industry Bank of Finland	Automatic		
Investments by Established Companies	Foreign-owned or controlled companies not permitted or allowed a limited participation only -- in the following sectors:	Forestry and forest industries, mining, real estate, agriculture, trade in securities, auditing firms, estate agencies, printing and publishing, employment agencies, accommodation and catering			For real estate and scarce natural resources: to keep in domestic hands	

FINLAND

Category	Measure	Sector	Authority/ Administration	Automatic/ Discretionary	Motivation/ Results	Other Information
		services, ship brokerage and forwarding, energy produc- tion.				
Investments by Established Companies	Government authorisation is required for foreign-controlled enterprises to purchase (or lease for more than two years) real estate.	All	Ministry of Trade and Industry	Automatic		
Investments by Established Companies	Limitations are placed on the capital of and on access to central bank credit by foreign-owned banks.	Banking	Bank of Finland	Automatic		This measure is temporary.
Investments by Established Companies	Foreign ownership in Finnish commer- cial banks, mortgage banks and finance companies is generalled limited.	Banking/Finance	Ministry of Finance Council of State	Automatic		
Investments by Established Companies	Non-national airlines are not permit- ted to carry passengers from one national point to another.	Air transporta- tion	National Board of Aviation/Council of State	Automatic		
Investments by Established Companies	Ships registered in Finland must be 60 per cent locally-owned. However, Finnish authorities have discretion to grant Finnish nationality to a vessel if its operation is Finnish to a decisive degree (though this power has never been used).	Maritime transportation				

FINLAND: TRANSPARENCY

Category	Measure	Sector	Authority/ Administration	Automatic/ Discretionary	Motivation/ Results	Other Information
Investments by Established Companies	Restrictions (usually less than 20 per cent ownership) apply to several sectors.	Ship registration, coastal shipping, land transportation, credit information, publishing defence material, surveillance services.	Ministry of Trade and Industry	Discretionary	National security (public order for surveillance services)	
Corporate Organisation	Nationality requirements are applied to founders, directors and officers under the Companies Act.	All	Ministry of Trade and Industry			

FRANCE

Category	Measure	Sector	Authority/ Administration	Automatic/ Discretionary	Motivation/ Results	Other Information
Official Aids and Subsidies	None.					
Tax Obligations	None.					
Access to Financing	None.					
Government Procurement	Preferential treatment is accorded to locally-owned firms in procurement for the armed forces.	Defence				
Government Procurement	Requirements for government employees to use national airlines/ferry services.	Tourism				
Investments by Established Companies	Foreign-controlled enterprises may acquire a locally-owned company only after receiving permission from the Ministry of Finance.	All				
Investments by Established Companies	In general, prior authorisation of the Ministre de l'Economie et des Finances is required for the making of direct investments by companies in France that are under direct or indirect foreign control, or by the establishments of foreign companies in France. (Decrees No. 67-68 of 27th January 1967 and No. 68-1021 of 24th November 1968).	All				
Investments by Established Companies	Prior authorisation is required for investment by French companies under Non-EEC control with certain exceptions for investments of less than FF 10 million per year.	All, except real estate				
Investments by Established Companies	Prior notification is required for investment by EEC-controlled enterprises, with certain exceptions.	All				

FRANCE

Category	Measure	Sector	Authority/Administration	Automatic/Discretionary	Motivation/Results	Other Information
Investments by Established Companies	Reciprocity required for the conduct of certain service activities.	Banking and finance, law, accounting, securities broking				
Investments by Established Companies	Foreigners may hold shares or participate in the financing of publications issued in France only on the basis of reciprocity.	Publishing				
Investments by Established Companies	Activities in the area of road transportation and renting of vehicles prohibited to foreign-controlled companies except in the case of EEC nationals and on the basis of reciprocity.	Transport				
Investments by Established Companies	The French Government reserves the right to restrict the right of establishment in the first and second degrees, and the conditions under which nationals or companies of other Member countries may carry on business connected with the production or processing of agricultural products, the acquisition of agricultural land and, in general, any activity which might endanger the security of France's food supply.	Agriculture				
Investments by Established Companies	Enterprises with head offices in non-EEC countries must obtain a licence to operate in France. The licence is granted only for types of insurance underwritten by the enterprise concerned in its country of origin.	Insurance				
Investments by Established Companies	Limitation on access to airline reservation systems.	Air transportation				
Investments by Established Companies	The National Treatment principle does not apply to companies, firms or other legal entities wishing to establish themselves in France for the purpose	Maritime transportation				

82

FRANCE

Category	Measure	Sector	Authority/ Administration	Automatic/ Discretionary	Motivation/ Results	Other Information
	of carrying on transit operations in connection with shipping, or having a controlling or participating interest in shipping either directly or by means of charter.					
Investments by Established Companies	Ships registered in France must be 50 per cent locally owned.	Maritime transportation				
Investments by Established Companies	Commercial transport of passengers and freight between any two points on French metropolitan or overseas territory is reserved to French aircraft, subject to any special temporary provisions that may be made by decree. Only undertakings whose principal business activity is air transport and whose head offices are in the territory of the French Republic may be authorised to carry on air transport business or establish regular airlines. Such undertakings must also meet certain requirements as to nationality (50 per cent of capital to be held by French associates or shareholders; nationality of certain executives).	Air transportation	Articles L. 330-2 and R. 330-2 of the Code de l'Aviation Civile			
Investments by Established Companies	Airfields intended for public use may be erected by individuals or legal entites meeting similar requirements as to nationality.	Airfields	Article D 221-1 of the Civil Aviation Code)			
Investments by Established Companies	The French Government reserves the right to restrict the conditions on which enterprises under foreign control and engaged in aircraft construction may be created or extended and may conduct business.	Aircraft construction				
Investments by Established Companies	National treatment is not applicable to the undertakings of the Commissariat à l'Energie Atomique, by virtue	Atomic Energy				

Category	Measure	Sector	Authority/Administration	Automatic/Discretionary	Motivation/Results	Other Information
	of Decree No. 70-878 of 29 September 1970, Article 2.					
	The following are excluded from the scope of application of National Treatment and are governed by a system of prior authorisation:					
	-- The use of artificial radioelements (Article 632 of the Code de la Santé Publique);					
	-- The operation of large nuclear plants;					
	-- Installations dealing with liquid radioactive waste from such plants (Decree of 31.12.1974).					
	The French Government expressly reserves the right to amend the regulations governing nuclear activities, and in particular the issue of uranium mining rights and permission to hold or make use of fissile materials.					
Investments by Established Companies	Coastal trade reserved to national flag carriers.	Maritime transportation				
Investments by Established Companies	Non-national airlines are not permitted to carry passengers from one national point to another.	Air transportation				
Investments by Established Companies	Non-national airlines not permitted to establish their own ground handling facilities.	Air transportation				

FRANCE: TRANSPARENCY

Category	Measure	Sector	Authority/ Administration	Automatic/ Discretionary	Motivation/ Results	Other Information
Government Procurement	The French Government will remain free to pursue the policy concerning defence equipment contracts that it considers best suited to the interests of national defence.	Defence			National defence	
Investments by Established Companies	The principle of national treatment is in no way applicable to enterprises concerned directly or indirectly with national defence or defence equipment.	Defence			National defence	
	In sectors that are directly or indirectly concerned with national defence or defence equipment, the French Government reserves the right to take all necessary steps to restrict the conditions of creation, extension, or conduct of business of entreprises under foreign control, or alternatively to obtain from such enterprises whatever guarantees it considers necessary.					
Corporate Organisation	The legal articles of co-operative association in agriculture provide that the administrators chosen from among the co-operating associates must be French nationals, or nationals of a Member State of the European Economic Community, or nationals of a country with which there is a reciprocity agreement, or must enjoy a derogation granted by the Minister of Agriculture on the advice of the Commission Centrale d'Agrément (vide Article 20 of Decree No. 59-286 of 4th February 1959 as amended by Decree No. 61-867 of 5th August 1961, Decree No. 69-821 of 28th August 1969 and Decree No. 73-1024 of 7th November 1973).	Food and Agriculture				

GERMANY

Category	Measure	Sector	Authority/Administration	Automatic/Discretionary	Motivation/Results	Other Information
Official Aids and Subsidies	None.					
Tax Obligations	None.					
Access to Financing	None.					
Government Procurement	The post office (DBP) purchases certain telecommunications equipment (including radio relay units and cables) mainly from locally-owned companies.	Telecommunications equipment	Federal Ministry of Posts and Telecommunications	Discretionary	To protect locally-owned companies while the international discussions on the opening of markets is continuing.	
Government Procurement	Requirements for government employees to use national airlines for official travel.	Air transportation	Federal Ministry of the Interior	Discretionary	Long-established practice that is to a very broad extent in accordance with the practice of other countries.	
Investments by Established Companies	The right to fly the German flag is reserved for ships owned by companies controlled by German nationals.	Maritime transportation	Federal Ministry of Transport	Automatic	In order to enable the control required by Article 5, paragraph I of the High Seas Convention.	
Investments by Established Companies	Coastal trade reserved to national flag carriers.	Maritime transportation	Federal Ministry of Transport	Discretionary	According to international customary law.	
Investments by Established Companies	A licence to operate an airline is granted only to companies majority controlled by German nationals.	Air transportation	Federal Ministry of Transport	Automatic	To comply with obligations spelt out in the ICAO agreement.	
Investments by Established Companies	Non-national airlines are not permitted to carry passengers from one national point to another.	Air transportation	Federal Ministry of Transport	Discretionary	A practice that is to a very broad extent in accordance with the practice of other countries.	

GERMANY: TRANSPARENCY

Category	Measure	Sector	Authority/ Administration	Automatic/ Discretionary	Motivation/ Results	Other Information
Official Aids and Subsidies	Provision of financial assistance and guarantees that exclude branches of foreign-controlled corporations.	Tourism				
Investments by Established Companies	Certain types of banking business can be conducted only by subsidiary companies, not branches of foreign credit institutions.	Banking	Federal Banking Supervisory Office	Automatic	Protection of the clients.	
Investments by Established Companies	Administrative practice confines the lead management of domestic currency issues by non-resident borrowers to banks incorporated in the Federal Republic of Germany. There is a voluntary gentleman's agreement between the Deutsche Bundesbank and the most important German banks on the issuing of foreign DM bonds. Inter alia, these banks have agreed to syndicate and sell foreign DM bonds on condition that a domestic bank acts as lead manager.	Investment Banking			To assure orderly domestic bond markets and allow monetary policy an influence on issue volume, given the increasing use of DMs as denomination currency.	

Category	Measure	Sector	Authority/ Administration	Automatic/ Discretionary	Motivation/ Results	Other Information
Official Aids and Subsidies	None.					
Tax Obligations	None.					
Access to Financing	None.					
Government Procurement	Government employees required to use national airlines when possible.	Air transportation				
Investments by Established Companies	Foreign ownership of Greek vessels restricted to 49 per cent and restrictions on maritime transport between Greek ports.	Maritime transportation				
Investments by Established Companies	Foreign investments involving the acquisition of real estate in border regions may be restricted.	All				
Investments by Established Companies	Foreign-controlled companies generally restricted to 40 per cent of capital of a bank established in Greece.	Banking				
Investments by Established Companies	Limitations on the placement of imported capital by foreign banks.	Banking				
Investments by Established Companies	Concession required for mining and mineral rights.	Mining				
Investments by Established Companies	Special restrictions apply to the purchase of land by established foreign-controlled companies in border regions.	Real Estate				
Investments by Established Companies	Coastal trade reserved to national flag carrier.	Maritime transportation				
Investments by Established Companies	Restrictions on coastal trade include certain voyages in which legs involving foreign ports are concerned.	Maritime transportation				

GREECE

Category	Measure	Sector	Authority/ Administration	Automatic/ Discretionary	Motivation/ Results	Other Information
Investments by Established Companies	Non-national airlines are not permitted to carry passengers from one national point to another.	Air transportation				
Foreign Exchange Controls	Limitations on the placement of import capital by foreign banks. Transfer restrictions applying to claims which are not based on the remittance of convertible currencies.					

GREECE: TRANSPARENCY

Category	Measure	Sector	Authority/ Administration	Automatic/ Discretionary	Motivation/ Results	Other Information
Government Procurement	Insurance of state property reserved to state-owned companies.	Insurance				
Tax Obligations	National carrier granted concessional income tax rate.	Tourism				
Corporate Organisation	Special requirements referring to nationality of directors.	Banks				

ICELAND

Category	Measure	Sector	Authority/ Administration	Automatic/ Discretionary	Motivation/ Results	Other Information
Official Aids and Subsidies	Provision of financial assistance and guarantees.	Tourism				
Tax Obligations	None.					
Access to Financing	None.					
Government Procurement	None.					
Investments by Established Companies	Non-national airlines are not permitted to carry passengers from one national point to another.	Air transportation				
Investments by Established Companies	Ships registered in Iceland must be 60 per cent locally owned.	Maritime transportation				

ICELAND: TRANSPARENCY

Category	Measure	Sector	Authority/ Administration	Automatic/ Discretionary	Motivation/ Results	Other Information

No measures reported under transparency.

IRELAND

Category	Measure	Sector	Authority/ Administration	Automatic/ Discretionary	Motivation/ Results	Other Information
Official Aids and Subsidies	None.					
Tax Obligations	None.					
Access to Financing	Prior Exchange Control permission is required for bank loans in Irish pounds.	All	Exchange controls are administered by the Central Bank of Ireland.	Permission is normally granted for enterprises controlled by residents of other EEC Member States to obtain all the Irish pound finance they require. Permission will normally be given to other foreign-controlled companies for funds required for working capital purposes.	It is expected that fixed asset financing would be contributed in the form of equity or loan capital from outside the State.	
Government Procurement	None.					
Investments by Established Companies	To be eligible for registration, sea fishing vessels must a) be owned by an Irish citizen or company and b) licensed to fish within the exclusive fishery limits of the State.	Fishing	Department of Fisheries and Forestry			Vessels of 60ft. and under are exempted from the licensing conditions.
Investments by Established Companies	Non-national airlines are not permitted to carry passengers from one national point to another.	Air transportation	Department of Transport			According to the Irish authorities, Ireland in accordance with Article 7 of the Chicago Convention does not permit non-national airlines to take on in its territory passenger mail and cargo destined for another point within its territory. However, airlines may carry passengers from one national point to

IRELAND

Category	Measure	Sector	Authority/ Administration	Automatic/ Discretionary	Motivation/ Results	Other Information
						another, in circumstances where the passengers are already on the aircraft and have travelled from an external point or where passengers are enroute to an external point.

IRELAND: TRANSPARENCY

Category	Measure	Sector	Authority/ Administration	Automatic/ Discretionary	Motivation/ Results	Other Information

No measures reported under transparency.

ITALY

Category	Measure	Sector	Authority/ Administration	Automatic/ Discretionary	Motivation/ Results	Other Information
Official Aids and Subsidies	Aids and subsidies are available for italian film production or co-production with foreign-controlled firms belonging to countries which have co-production agreements with Italy. Subsidies may also be available for the processing and the distribution of films by Italian-owned companies.	Films	Ministry of Tourism and Shows	Automatic/ Discretionary		Unlimited duration
Tax Obligations	None.					
Access to Financing	Foreign-controlled enterprises may borrow locally on medium and long-term only up to 50 per cent of the capital must be brought into Italy; such borrowing notified to the Italian Ministry of the Treasury.	All	Ministry of the Treasury Law of 7/2/56, No. 43	Automatic		
Government Procurement	Recommendation for government employees travelling abroad under the budget of the Ministry of Foreign Affairs to use the national airlines.	Air transportation	Ministry of Foreign Affairs Circular of 15/3/78	Discretionary		
Investments by Established Companies	The authority for non-EEC banks to establish branches is subject to the principle of reciprocity.	Banking	Treasury Ministry Ministry of Foreign Affairs Ministerial Committee for Credit and Saving R.D. No. 1620 of 4/9/19	Automatic/ Discretionary		Unlimited duration
Investments by Established Companies	Branches of foreign banks may freely grant loans which do not exceed 3/5 of their own capital. Loans over this limit must be authorised by the Bank of Italy; no ceiling is envisaged for authorised credits which exceed 3/5 of capital.	Banking	Bank of Italy	Automatic/ Discretionary		
Investments by Established Companies	Branches of foreign banks established in Italy may grant loans in the region in which they are located and in all of Italy in cases of loans extended to foreign enterprises or to subsidiaries of such enterprises.	Banking	Bank of Italy	Automatic/ Discretionary		

Category	Measure	Sector	Authority/ Administration	Automatic/ Discretionary	Motivation/ Results	Other Information
Investments by Established Companies	Ownership by foreign-controlled enterprises or citizens of ships is possible if the ships are owned over 50 per cent, or 12 carats by 1) Italian citizens; 2) Italian public institutions; and 3) companies established and head quartered in Italy or private institutions whose capital and managers are over 50 per cent Italian. In this case, exceptionally, it is possible for reasons of national security to grant Italian nationality to companies created above which, however, have their headquarters or main activity in Italy.	Shipping	Ministry of Merchant Marines	Automatic/ Discretionary		
Investments by Established Companies	Cabotage in Italian ports as well as maritime services of the ports, the road steads, and the beaches are reserved for Italian-owned ships, unless international conventions indicate otherwise.	Maritime trans-portation	Ministry of Merchant Marine	Automatic		
Investments by Established Companies	Fishing in territorial waters is reserved for Italian citizens.	Fishing	Ministry of Merchant Marine	Automatic		
Investments by Established Companies	For non-EEC insurance companies, the principle of reciprocity applies and for foreign enterprises, the general representative in Italy must be an Italian citizen residing in Italy.	Insurance	Ministry of Industry			
Investments by Established Companies	Air transportation services within Italy (cabotage) are reserved for nationals unless international conventions state otherwise. Such activities could be undertaken by foreign-controlled companies if the Chief of State grants permission, based on public interest reasons.	Air transporta-tion	Ministry of Transportation	Automatic/ Discretionary		
Investments by Established Companies	Ownership of national aircrafts (i.e. aircrafts registered in the national aeronautic register) is reserved for:	Air transport				

ITALY

Category	Measure	Sector	Authority/ Administration	Automatic/ Discretionary	Motivation/ Results	Other Information
	a) State, provinces, communes and other Italian public institutions; b) Italian citizens; c) Category whose capital is owned at least two-thirds by Italian citizens and two-thirds of the directors, including delegated directors, and the director general are Italians.					
Investments by Established Companies	Non-national airlines not permitted to establish their own ground handling facilities.	Air transportation	Ministry of Transportation			

ITALY: TRANSPARENCY

Category	Measure	Sector	Authority/ Administration	Automatic/ Discretionary	Motivation/ Results	Other Information

No measures reported under transparency.

JAPAN

Category	Measure	Sector	Authority/Administration	Automatic/Discretionary	Motivation/Results	Other Information
Official Aids and Subsidies	None.					
Tax Obligations	None.					
Access to Financing	None.					
Government Procurement	None.					
Investments by Established Companies	Foreign-controlled enterprises (where capital ownership exceeds 50 per cent or a majority of the board of directors is non-resident in Japan) must provide prior notification to increase their capital investment or change the activities of their business. Such changes are approved, unless the government provides notice to the contrary in 30 days.	All	Minister of Finance and Ministry responsible for the sector concerned.	Automatic		Law: Foreign Exchange and Foreign Trade Control Law.
Investments by Established Companies	Foreign-controlled enterprises may be restricted from engaging in certain sectors of business activity in accordance with Japanese law.	Agriculture, fisheries, forestry, mining, oil industry, leather and leather products.	Minister of Finance and Ministry responsible for the sector concerned.	Discretionary	The government's national resources and employment policy.	Law: Foreign Exchange and Foreign Trade Control Law.
Investments by Established Companies	Non-national airlines are not permitted to carry passengers from one national point to another.	Air transportation				

JAPAN: TRANSPARENCY

Category	Measure	Sector	Authority/ Administration	Automatic/ Discretionary	Motivation/ Results	Other Information
Investments by Established Companies	No foreign corporation or Japanese corporation with more than one-third foreign ownership can register aircraft.	Air transporta- tion	Air transporta- tion Law Article 4		National security and public order	
Investments by Established Companies	No foreign corporation or Japanese corporation with more than one-third foreign ownership can have a licence for a radio station.	Radio broad- casting			National security and public order	
Investments by Established Companies	No foreign corporation or Japanese corporation with more than one-fifth foreign ownership may receive a licence for cable television broadcasting.	Cable television broadcasting			National security and public order	
Investments by Established Companies	Foreign-controlled enterprises may be restricted from engaging in certain business activities related to natio- nal security and maintenance of the public order in accordance with related Japanese law.	Atomic energy, arms manufacture, narcotics	Minister of Finance and Ministry of sector conerned.	Automatic	National security and public order	

101

LUXEMBOURG

Category	Measure	Sector	Authority/ Administration	Automatic/ Discretionary	Motivation/ Results	Other Information
Official Aids and Subsidies	None.					
Tax Obligations	None.					
Access to Financing	None.					
Government Procurement	None.					
Investments by Established Companies	Take over bids by established non-EEC foreign-controlled enterprises must be approved.	All				
Investments by Established Companies	Some restrictions apply to foreign-controlled companies.	Public transport and regularly scheduled air transport				
Investments by Established Companies	Non-national airlines are not permitted to carry passengers from one national point to another.	Air transportation				

LUXEMBOURG: TRANSPARENCY

Category	Measure	Sector	Authority/ Administration	Automatic/ Discretionary	Motivation/ Results	Other Information

No measures reported under transparency.

Category	Measure	Sector	Authority/ Administration	Automatic/ Discretionary	Motivation/ Results	Other Information
Official Aids and Subsidies	None.					
Tax Obligations	None.					
Access to Financing	None.					
Government Procurement	Government employees urged to use national airlines.	Tourism				
Investments by Established Companies	The Netherlands flag is reserved for ships owned by companies that are two-thirds owned by Dutch nationals.	Maritime transportation	Directorate General for Shipping and Maritime Affairs	Automatic	To ensure compliance with Dutch safety standards and laws pertaining to social security, taxation and industrial relations.	
Investments by Established Companies	A licence to operate an airline based in the Netherlands is generally granted only to enterprises which are under Dutch control or Dutch management.	Air transportation	Department of Civil Aviation		To ensure compliance with Dutch safety standards and laws pertaining to social security, taxation and industrial relations.	
Investments by Established Companies	Non-national airlines are not permitted to carry passengers from one national point to another.	Air transportation	Department of Civil Aviation		Considerations of reciprocity	

NETHERLANDS: TRANSPARENCY

Category	Measure	Sector	Authority/ Administration	Automatic/ Discretionary	Motivation/ Results	Other Information
Investments by Established Companies	The government reserves the right to prohibit foreign companies from producing defence supplies in particular cases.	Defence			National security	
Investments by Established Companies	Branches of foreign enterprises are not permitted to act as lead managers of underwritings of securities issues in local currency on the local capital market.	Investment Banking				
Corporate Management	Foreign nationals must apply for a work permit.	All	Ministry of Social Affairs	Discretionary	To ensure employee will have a benefi- cial impact in gene- ral and is essential to the company.	

NEW ZEALAND

Category	Measure	Sector	Authority/ Administration	Automatic/ Discretionary	Motivation/ Results	Other Information
Official Aids and Subsidies	Tax incentives not available to non-residents.	Mining				
Official Aids and Subsidies	Provision of financial assistance and guarantees.	Tourism				
Tax Obligations	Special treatment for branches: -- Higher rate of income tax; -- Higher rates of land tax for absentee individuals and share-holders; -- Assessment of taxable income from films, insurance and shipping; -- Tax collection.	All				
Access to Financing	Authorisation required where 25 per cent or more of a New Zealand company is under foreign control.	All				
Government Procurement	Requirements for government employees to use national airlines/ferry services.	Tourism				
Investments by Established Companies	The approval for establishment of a foreign-owned merchant bank is subject to local equity participation.	Banking	Overseas Investment Commission	Discretionary		
Investments by Established Companies	Investment by foreign-controlled enterprises requires authorisation by the Overseas Investment Commission.	All				
Investments by Established Companies	Authorisation is required for take-overs or expansion into non-related areas.	All				
Investments by Established Companies	Foreign transportation firms welcome only if the economy benefits in terms of transporting more people into and around the country.	Tourism				
Investments by Established Companies	Specific provisions apply.	Land ownership; shipping				

106

NEW ZEALAND

Category	Measure	Sector	Authority/ Administration	Automatic/ Discretionary	Motivation/ Results	Other Information
Investments by Established Companies	Coastal trade reserved to national flag carriers.	Maritime trans- portation				
Investments by Established Companies	Non-national airlines are not permit- ted to carry passengers from one national point to another.	Air transporta- tion				

NEW ZEALAND: TRANSPARENCY

Category	Measure	Sector	Authority/ Administration	Automatic/ Discretionary	Motivation/ Results	Other Information

No measures reported under transparency.

Category	Measure	Sector	Authority/Administration	Automatic/Discretionary	Motivation/Results	Other Information
Official Aids and Subsidies	None.					
Tax Obligations	None.					
Access to Financing	None.					
Government Procurement	None.					
Investments by Established Companies	Norwegian corporations, where more than 20 per cent of share capital or voting rights is controlled by foreign persons or foreign-controlled companies or where one member of the board is an alien, must have a concession to conduct business operations or to acquire Norwegian companies. Concession terms (conditions) are stipulated in connection with the concession. It is thus usually required that the Chairman and the majority of the Board of Directors are Norwegian citizens, and that transactions between the Norwegian subsidiary and its foreign parent company are based upon realistic pricing and optimum conditions for the Norwegian company. Agreements between subsidiary and parent firms regarding payments for economic, technical, mercantile and other assistance must also be approved by the Norwegian authorities. The conditions may also regulate the type of production, financing terms and other circumstances, varying from company to company.	All	Concession Act of 14/12/17 Ministry of Industry	Discretionary	General regulation of the exploitation of national resources.	
Investments by Established Companies	Foreign investment in banks limited to 10 per cent, or 25 per cent with prior authorisation.	Banking	Act relating to Commercial Banks Norway of 24/5/61 Ministry of Finance	Automatic/ Discretionary	Hinder establishment by foreign banks (legislation under reconsideration).	

Category	Measure	Sector	Authority/ Administration	Automatic/ Discretionary	Motivation/ Results	Other Information
Investments by Established Companies	Foreign-controlled companies must have a concession to acquire real property or more than 10 per cent of the share capital of a company owning or leasing real property.	All	Concession Act of 14/12/17. Ministry of Industry			
Investments by Established Companies	Corporations having their seat in Norway and an executive board where the majority of the members, including the Chairman, are Norwegian citizens, may obtain a concession to purchase electric power in larger quantities than 500 kW. If the concessionmaire is a corporation with an executive board which is not entirely Norwegian or a basic capital which is not entirely Norwegian held, the State may in the concession terms reserve a right to purchase, not later than 40 years from the concession date, the factory plants established for the purpose of utilising the power, together with land, buildings, machinery, facilities etc.	All, purchase of electric power				
Investments by Established Companies	The establishment of travel agencies is subject to concession which can be granted to enterprises where six-tenths of the equity capital is owned by Norwegian nationals and where two-thirds of the board members are Norwegian nationals.	Travel agenices	Travel Agency Act of 12/6/81 Ministry of Communications		In the absence of such requirements concerning natio-nality of equity and board members Norwegian control-led enterprises might be placed at a competitive disadvantage com-pared to big foreign-controlled enterprises and there might be a tendency towards fewer and bigger agencies through mergers and acquisitions.	

Category	Measure	Sector	Authority/ Administration	Automatic/ Discretionary	Motivation/ Results	Other Information
Investments by Established Companies	As a rule fishing is reserved for Norwegian nationals and corporations where all members of the Board are Norwegian nationals and at least six tenths of the equity capital is controlled by Norwegian nationals. However, under special circumstances permits may be granted to other corporations.	Fishing	Fishing Limit Act of 17/6/66 Ministry of Fishing	Discretionary	National control of natural resources	
Investments by Established Companies	Registration of ships in Norway and ownership of ships flying the Norwegian flag are in principle reserved for Norwegian nationals and companies where at least six-tenths of the shares are owned by Norwegian nationals.	Shipping	Maritime Act of 20/7/1893 Ministry of Commerce and Shipping	Automatic	Genuine link between ownership and nationality of ships. Practised liberally. Dispensations frequently granted.	
Investments by Established Companies	Establishment and operation of free warehouses, free ports, etc. may be limited to Norwegian-owned companies.	Warehousing, free ports	Customs Act of 10/6/66	Discretionary		
Investments by Established Companies	Non-national airlines are not permitted to carry passengers from one national point to another.	Air transportation	Civil Aviation Act of 16/12/60 Ministry of Communications			
Foreign exchange controls	Foreign-owned or controlled-enterprises are as a rule treated as residents with regard to foreign exchange control. However, according to the Currency Control Act, the Ministry of Finance may decide that such enterprises be treated as non-residents.	All	Currency Control Act 14/7/50 Ministry of Finance	Discretionary		

NORWAY: TRANSPARENCY

Category	Measure	Sector	Authority/ Administration	Automatic/ Discretionary	Motivation/ Results	Other Information
Official Aids and Subsidies	State-owned oil companies sometimes get exclusive or priority access to leases and concessions and preferential treatment in supplies or use of crude oil.	Oil Industry				
Investments by Established Companies	Foreign insurers operating in Norway are required to make an initial deposit as security for their operations (1).	Insurance	Insurance Companies Act of 29/7/11			According to the Norwegian authorities, there is a proposal to eliminate this measure.
Corporate Organisation	Certain Norwegian laws, notably the Companies Act, require that the manager or the board members shall be domiciled in the country. Other laws require in addition that such persons must have resided in the country for a certain period. For certain liberal professions there are requirements concerning residence in the country, education and practice. Certain operations require that the corporation must have an executive board where the board members are Norwegian citizens (acquisition of water falls and mines, prospection and mining of ores and metals). Provisions concerning the nationality of employees are found in specific sectors (aviation, shipping).	All/specific sectors		Automatic		

1. The Committee left open the question of whether such measure is a condition of establishment and therefore outside the scope of the National Treatment instrument.

112

PORTUGAL

Category	Measure	Sector	Authority/Administration	Automatic/Discretionary	Motivation/Results	Other Information
Official Aids and Subsidies	National carrier exempt from stamp taxes on revenue receipts.	Air transportation	Director General of Taxes	Automatic	The crisis of the sector.	
Tax Obligations	None.					
Access to Financing	1) No restrictions on short-term (up to one year) borrowing from ordinary credit institutions.	All except investment and financial leasing companies	Bank of Portugal Institute of Foreign Investment	Discretionary for exceeding limits, for branches and for access to special public credit institutions	While recognising the advantages of foreign investment for Portuguese development, such development requires that limitations be placed on such investment and it is expected that foreign investment projects will not be financed predominantly from local bank credit.	
	2) If foreign ownership of a locally incorporated enterprise is between 25 per cent and 50 per cent of its capital, the firm can borrow from these institutions medium-term up to 70 per cent of the net worth of the firm.					
	3) If foreign ownership exceeds 50 per cent, the firm can borrow medium term from these institutions, up to 50 per cent of its net worth. However, with prior authorisation these limits may be exceeded, and long-term borrowing may be authorised.					
	4) Branches in Portugal of foreign enterprises may borrow, medium and long-term, with prior approval.	All				
	5) Foreign-owned enterprises or branches of foreign companies may have access to credit from special public sources upon conditions to be fixed by the government.	All				
Government Procurement	1) With the exceptions noted below, public works contracts may be undertaken only by Portuguese companies where the majority of the shareholders are Portuguese and 60 per cent of capital is held by Portuguese.	All except electrical and mechnical equipment installation	Ministry of Public Works	Automatic	Reserving public works projects for locally-owned companies is a means to protect the public interest. However, the need	

Category	Measure	Sector	Authority/ Administration	Automatic/ Discretionary	Motivation/ Results	Other Information
	2) For electrical and mechanical equipment installation contracts, foreign-owned companies qualify whose headquarters are in Portugal and who have operated their principal activity in Portugal for at least two years.	Electrical and mechanical equipment installation		Automatic	for electrical and mechanical technology has liberalised public contracts in this area.	
	3) If a solicitation for bids in public works does not receive an adequate response or if the characteristics of the project justify such a measure, foreign-owned enterprises may be invited to bid.	All	The Ministry soliciting tenders	Discretionary		
Investments by Established Companies	Under Decree Law 174/82 amending Decree Law 348/77, investments by companies established in Portugal with foreign capital that have more than 25 per cent foreign-owned capital, that result in acquisition of more than 50 per cent of the capital of another company established in Portugal, are subject to prior approval, as are investments resulting in any percentage of ownership of companies holding or operating public property or public services under Decree Law 46312/65. Changes of articles of association of companies established in Portugal that result in a change in their purpose or their majority ownership are also subject to prior approval.	All	Institute of Foreign Investment	Discretionary	To follow the importance of foreign investment in Portugal.	
Investments by Established Companies	Mining activities are permitted only to majority locally-owned companies unless the Council of Ministers decides otherwise.	Mining	Decree-Law 46312 of 28/4/65	Discretionary		Duration: under review
Investments by Established Companies	Limitations apply to activities of foreign-owned travel agencies.	Travel agencies				

114

Category	Measure	Sector	Authority/ Administration	Automatic/ Discretionary	Motivation/ Results	Other Information
Investments by Established Companies	A fixed percentage of certain imports is reserved to the national flag.	Maritime transportation	State Office of the Merchant Marine - Director General of Maritime Commerce	Automatic	Concern of developing the maritime transportation sector.	
Investments by Established Companies	International road transportation activities may be undertaken only by companies majority-owned and administered by nationals.	Road transportation	Decree-Law 477/71			Duration: under review
Investments by Established Companies	In the outward bound direction, foreign-controlled companies may not load passengers locally for the return leg except in exceptional cases.	Air transportation	Minister of Transportation	Automatic	International air convention provides the basis of this measure.	
Investments by Established Companies	Non-national airlines are not permitted to carry passengers from one national point to another.	Air transportation			In accordance with the International Air Convention of 1944.	
Investments by Established Companies	Non-regularly scheduled airlines must be majority-owned and administered by nationals.	Air transportation	Decree-Law 19/82	Automatic		Duration: under review
Investments by Established Companies	Investments by foreign-owned companies in companies that publish periodicals cannot exceed 10 per cent, without voting rights.	Publishing	Decree-Law 85-C/75	Automatic		Duration: under review
Investments by Established Companies	Foreign-owned companies may not own a majority interest in insurance brokerage companies and the managers must be nationals.	Insurance Brokerage	Decree-Law 145/79	Automatic		Duration: under review
Investments by Established Companies	Companies must be 60 per cent owned and administered by nationals.	Maritime transportation for tourism	Decree-Law 19/78	Automatic		Duration: under review

PORTUGAL: TRANSPARENCY

Category	Measure	Sector	Authority/ Administration	Automatic/ Discretionary	Motivation/ Results	Other Information
Investments by Established Companies	Coastal trade reserved to companies owned 60 per cent by nationals.	Maritime trans- portation	Decree-Law 135/72 State Office of the Merchant Marine - Director General of Maritime Commerce	Discretionary	National security	Duration under review
Investments by Established Companies	Public services (including national defence), basic industries, public property are part of the public sec- tor and are generally not subject to acquisition or exploitation by compa- nies which are majority-owned by foreign individuals or companies. The Council of Ministers may authorise exceptions to this policy, as has been done in the mining sector. While basic industries (like arms manufac- turing, petroleum refining, petro- chemicals, steel) are reserved to the State, minority participation in these sectors by foreign-owned companies may be of interest to the country.	Various	Council of Ministers	Discretionary	Public security and interest. National measures and government policies.	

SPAIN

Category	Measure	Sector	Authority/Administration	Automatic/Discretionary	Motivation/Results	Other Information
Official Aids and Subsidies	Provision of financial assistance and guarantees.	Tourism				
Tax Obligations	None.					
Access to Financing	None.					
Government Procurement	None.					
Investments by Established Companies	Foreign-controlled enterprises who wish to control more than 50 per cent of a Spanish enterprise must apply for authorisation.	All				
Investments by Established Companies	Foreign-owned banks in Spain are restricted in the number of branches (presently two) they can open.	Banking				
Investments by Established Companies	Foreign-owned banks in Spain may not borrow (other than on the interbank market) domestically more than 40 per cent of total assets, unless specially authorised.	Banking	Bank of Spain	Discretionary		
Investments by Established Companies	Foreign-owned banks' securities portfolio must generally consist of only government bonds.	Banking	Bank of Spain Ministry of the Economy	Automatic		
Investments by Established Companies	Special restrictions to participation by foreign-controlled companies.	National defense, armament, nuclear industries, public services, air transport, shipping, mining, broadcasting, banks, film industries, news-papers and news agencies, conces-sions for the exploitation of water resources, casinos.				

117

SPAIN

Category	Measure	Sector	Authority/ Administration	Automatic/ Discretionary	Motivation/ Results	Other Information
Investments by Established Companies	A fixed percentage of certain imports is reserved to the national flag.	Maritime trans- portation				
Investments by Established Companies	Coastal trade reserved to national flag carriers.	Maritime trans- portation				
Investments by Established Companies	Restrictions on coastal trade include certain voyages in which legs involv- ing foreign ports are concerned.	Maritime trans- portation				
Investments by Established Companies	Non-national airlines are not permit- ted to carry passengers from one national point to another.	Air transporta- tion				
Investments by Established Companies	Benefits (such as accommodation) offered by local tourist organisation to transatlantic passengers who use the national airline.	Air transporta- tion				
Investments by Established Companies	Non-national airlines not permitted to sell ground-handling services to other airlines.	Air transporta- tion				

SPAIN: TRANSPARENCY

Category	Measure	Sector	Authority/ Administration	Automatic/ Discretionary	Motivation/ Results	Other Information

No measures reported under transparency.

Category	Measure	Sector	Authority/ Administration	Automatic/ Discretionary	Motivation/ Results	Other Information
Official Aids and Subsidies	None.					
Tax Obligations	None.					
Access to Financing	Authorisation from the Riksbank is required when domestic loans are granted against the guarantee of a non-resident. The practice of the Riksbank with regard to the authorisation of loans to established foreign-owned companies against the guarantee of non-residents, in the case of financing of investment in fixed assets, normally implies that at least 50 per cent of the part of the investment which corresponds to the foreign interest in the enterprise has to be financed by transfers of funds from abroad. Investments amounting to less than SKR 5 million are exempted. Lending against the guarantee of a non-resident for acquisition of working capital is normally permitted.	All	Law	Discretionary	The general reason for exchange control is due to the need to have a bona-fide control, i.e. that the applicant is going to make a direct and not a portfolio investment. The particular reason for requesting foreign financing has to do with balance of payment and the limited size of the Swedish credit market.	
Government Procurement	None.					
Investments by Established Companies	Acquisition of real property. Aliens and foreign corporations (including Swedish legal entities with the status of foreign corporations) must have a special permit to acquire real property. Such a permit is generally granted when the property is needed for the activities of the enterprise. Also the right to claim mineral deposits, to acquire or work claimed mineral deposits or engage in mining requires a special permit. (If mining rights are wholly or partially held by virtue of such a permit, the Government can demand the compulsory sales of the rights to the State or to some other entity, in	All, including mining (except insurance companies)	Law	Discretionary	To protect natural resources	

120

Category	Measure	Sector	Authority/ Administration	Automatic/ Discretionary	Motivation/ Results	Other Information
	situations where there are special reasons for securing Swedish control of the mining company. This provision has never been used).					
Investments by Established Companies	Establishing a subsidiary of a foreign-owned bank as well as acquisition of participations in Swedish banks by foreign-owned companies is not permitted.	Banking	Law	Automatic	Due to the essential role of Swedish banks for Swedish exchange controls and credit policy it has been considered important to prevent foreigners from having the possibility to obtain an influential position in these institutions.	
Investments by Established Companies	There has recently been imposed a temporary prohibition for foreign corporations and other control subjects, including Swedish corporations not having a foreigners' clause in their Articles of Association, to acquire shares in Swedish finance corporations or broker firms.	Finance, securities brokerage	Law	Automatic	This prohibition is expected to be temporary pending an official review of the structure of the Swedish credit market.	
Investments by Established Companies	Foreign corporations and Swedish corporations not having a "foreign ownership restriction clause" in their Articles of Association, may not acquire, without permission, shares in Swedish corporations and partnerships exceeding certain levels of the equity capital (10, 20, 40 and 50 per cent). A permit shall be granted if the acquisition is not in conflict with any essential public interest. In case any undertakings of importance to the decision to grant the permit have been made by the acquirer, such undertakings shall be mentioned in the decision. In practice, permits are granted liberally.	All except banking and insurance	Law	Discretionary	To protect public interest	

121

SWEDEN

Category	Measure	Sector	Authority/ Administration	Automatic/ Discretionary	Motivation/ Results	Other Information
Investments by Established Companies	Foreign participation restricted.	Domestic road transport services	Law		This restriction is based on general limitations on right of establishment	
Investments by Established Companies	Access to international air routes to or from Sweden are regulated by bilateral intergovernmental agreement.	Air transportation			This is in conformity with a universally applied practice.	
Investments by Established Companies	Non-national airlines are restricted in carriage of passengers from one national point to another.	Air transportation			Consistent with the Convention on International Civil Aviation (Chicago Convention).	

Category	Measure	Sector	Authority/ Administration	Automatic/ Discretionary	Motivation/ Results	Other Information
Tax Obligations	Branches in Sweden of foreign companies may not take a deduction from taxable income for dividends distributed (as may locally-incorporated companies) and may not allocate tax free amounts to investment funds or or deduct intra-group payments (as may locally-incorporated companies).	All	Law	Automatic	Branches in Sweden of foreign companies are not subject to economic double taxation in Sweden. Transfers of profits on activities in Sweden to the foreign head office do not give rise to taxation in Sweden.	
Investments by Established Companies	A government permit is required for both foreign-controlled and domestic enterprises to produce war-munitions in Sweden. In practice, a foreign-controlled enterprise is allowed to produce war-munitions only to a small extent.	War munitions	Law	Discretionary	For national security reasons	
Investments by Established Companies	In principle, a permit to conduct credit information activities must not be granted to foreign corporations or other control subjects, including Swedish corporations not having a foreigners' clause in their articles of association.	Credit information activities	Law		The reasons for this regulation are increased risks for personal integrity and national security due to foreign control of the credit information activities.	
Corporate management	In principle there are nationality requirements for directors, etc. in foreign-controlled as well as in limited corporations and co-operative societies. However, by means of a government permit, foreigners are generally allowed to assume such posts in the enterprises. In practice there is no discrimination between foreign-controlled and domestic enterprises.	All	Law	Discretionary	When allowing foreigners to assume such posts in the enterprise it must be proved that the applicants have a good knowledge of Swedish society and its customs.	

123

SWITZERLAND

Category	Measure	Sector	Authority/ Administration	Automatic/ Discretionary	Motivation/ Results	Other Information
Official Aids and Subsidies	Subsidies for motion picture production are only granted for films produced by Swiss companies, where foreign participation is less than 50 per cent unless there is reciprocal treatment in the country of the foreign shareholder.	Film production	Film Section; Federal Office of Cultural Affairs, DFI (1)	Automatic	To encourage Swiss film production	Law: RS 443.11 of 28/12/62
Tax Obligations	None.					
Access to Financing	None.					
Government Procurement	Requirements for government employees to use national airlines services.	Tourism	Federal Department of Finance			
Investments by Established Companies	Established foreign-owned companies acquisition of control of a Swiss bank or of a minority position in a Swiss bank controlled by foreigners is subject to reciprocity in the country of the acquirers and the name of such bank must not indicate that it is Swiss owned.	Banking	Federal Banking Commission	Automatic	To create opportunities for establishment of Swiss banks abroad, to guarantee the observation of the National Swiss Bank policy, and the protection of depositors.	Law: RS 952.0 of 8/11/34
Investments by Established Companies	Only Swiss-owned companies are permitted to distribute motion picture films in Switzerland.	Motion picture distribution	Film Section; Federal Office of Cultural Affairs, DFI	Automatic	To guarantee the independence of the Swiss film market.	Law: RS 443.1 of 28/9/62
Investments by Established Companies	If a foreign insurance company wishes to open a branch in Switzerland, it must have transacted insurance business for at least three years. The general agent of the branch must be a Swiss citizen; his nomination and	Insurance	Federal Office of Private Insurance, DFJP (2)	Automatic	Experience requirement is to protect policy holders from inexperienced companies.	Law: RS 961.01 of 23/6/78

1. Federal Department of the Interior.

2. Federal Department of Justice and Police.

124

Category	Measure	Sector	Authority/ Administration	Automatic/ Discretionary	Motivation/ Results	Other Information
	procuration must be approved by the Federal Office of Private Insurance. It must have an office in Switzerland for the totality of its Swiss activities.					
Investments by Established Companies	The Swiss branch of a foreign insurance company is subject to legal requirements for guaranties that are different from those applied to Swiss insurance companies.	Insurance	Federal Office of Private Insurance, DFJP		cf. above	Law: RS 961.02 of 4/2/19
Investments by Established Companies	With certain exceptions, an aeroplane can be registered in Switzerland only if exclusively owned by Swiss citizens or companies, constituted according to Swiss law and having their head office in Switzerland. Commercial air transportation between points in Switzerland is reserved to Swiss companies. Authorisation to provide commercial aviation services could be granted to foreign-owned enterprises if consistent with essential Swiss interests and if there is reciprocity in the foreign country concerned.	Air transportation	DFTCE (1)	Automatic/ Discretionary	The International Aviation Convention of 7/12/44 provides a basis for these measures. Essential national interests.	Law: RS 748.0 of 21/12/48

1. Federal Department of Transportation, Communications and Energy.

SWITZERLAND: TRANSPARENCY

Category	Measure	Sector	Authority/ Administration	Automatic/ Discretionary	Motivation/ Results	Other Information
Investments by Established Companies	A concession for the construction and operation of a pipeline that crosses the Swiss border, to transport flammable fuels or liquids or gas, is available only to Swiss companies not controlled by foreign interests.	Pipeline transmission	Federal Council	Automatic	National security	Law: RS 746.1 of 4/10/63
Investments by Established Companies	Certain activities are generally unavailable for foreign-controlled enterprises or available only by special concession because the Swiss Confederation or its Cantons holds a public monopoly.	Railroad transportation	DFTCE	Discretionary	National defence, protection of the environment, following obligations: -- Respect of timetable; -- Respect of tariff; -- Guarantee of operation; -- Transport of persons and goods.	Law: RS 742.101 of 20/12/57
		Internal navigation	DFTCE	Discretionary		Law: RS 747.201 of 3/10/75 and RS 747.211.1 of 9/8/72
		Postal service	DFTCE	Automatic	Security of operation, postal and telephone secrecy.	Law: RS 783.0 of 2/10/24
		Public, commercial automobile transportation	DFTCE	Discretionary	Following obligations: -- Respect of timetable; -- Respect of tariff; -- Transport of persons and goods; -- Guarantee of operation.	Law: RS 744.11 of 4/1/60

SWITZERLAND: TRANSPARENCY

Category	Measure	Sector	Authority/ Administration	Automatic/ Discretionary	Motivation/ Results	Other Information
		Cable car operation	DFTCE	Discretionary	Allocating land use, environmental protection and national defence.	Law: RS 743.11 of 8/11/78
		Telecommunications -- electric audio or video transmission	Federal Council	Automatic		Law: RS 784.10 of 14/10/22 and RS 784.401 of 7/6/82. Concessions may be granted for local radio transmission to Swiss controlled companies.
		Alcoholic beverages	Federal Alcohol Authority, DFF (1)	Discretionary	To safeguard public health	Law: RS 680 of 21/6/32 and article 32 bis of the Federal Constitution
		Explosives importation production sales	Federal Military Administration, DMF (2)	Discretionary	Security	Law: RS 941.41 of 25/3/77
		Bread flour importation	Federal Wheat Administration, DFEI (3)	Discretionary	Security of supply	Law: RS 916.111.0 of 20/3/59
		Fishing, hunting, mining, salt, fire insurance	Cantonal authorities			Cantonal monopolies in particular Cantons
Investments by Established Companies	Non-national airlines not permitted to establish their own ground-handling facilities.	Air transportation	Federal Office of Civil Aviation; DFTCE		Rights from the concession system	

1. DFF -- Federal Finance Department.
2. DMF -- Federal Military Department.
3. DFEP -- Department of Public Economy.

127

Category	Measure	Sector	Authority/Administration	Automatic/Discretionary	Motivation/Results	Other Information
Investments by Established Companies	Registration of ships that are engaged in the commercial transportation of goods or persons is granted only to companies whose capital is wholly owned by Swiss interests.	Maritime transportation	Swiss Office of Maritime Navigation	Automatic	The Swiss merchant fleet is to ensure service in times of international crisis. National security	Law: RS 747.3 of 23/9/53
Investments by Established Companies	A concession for utilising hydropower can be granted only to corporations with headquarters in Switzerland with two-thirds of the managers Swiss citizens domiciled in Switzerland.	Hydropower	Confederation, canton or commune	Automatic	National security, security of supply	Law: RS 721/80 of 22/12/16
Investments by Established Companies	An intercantonal agreement among ten cantons provides that a concession for petroleum production may be granted only to companies that are 75 per cent owned by Swiss interests.	Petroleum production	Cantonal authoritie	Automatic	National security	Law: RS 931.1 of 24/9/55
Investments by Established Companies	Authorisation to build and operate a nuclear plant is granted only to Swiss-controlled companies.	Nuclear energy	Federal Council. Authorisation granted by the Federal Assembly.	Automatic	To maintain independent production of electricity and to protect public health and safety. National security.	Law: RS 732.01 of 6/10/78
Investments by Established Companies	The acquisition of real property by foreign-controlled corporations is subject to authorisation of the Cantons. The approval should be granted if the purpose of the ownership of real property has a legitimate business purpose.	All	Cantonal authorities	Automatic	The scarcity of real estate in Switzerland and the great demand for it has caused a need to administer the use of real estate.	Law: RS 211.412.41 of 23/3/61
Corporate management	The board of directors of a corporation with limited liability in the form of an S.A. (except holding companies) must have a majority of Swiss citizens domiciled in Switzerland.	All	Commercial registry.	Automatic	To reinforce relationships between S.A. companies predominantly foreign-owned and Swiss authorities, in particular tax authorities.	Law: Article 711 of the Code of Obligations

TURKEY

Category	Measure	Sector	Authority/ Administration	Automatic/ Discretionary	Motivation/ Results	Other Information
Official Aids and Subsidies	Subsidisation of low fares for expatriation workers on national carrier.	Air transportation				
Official Aids and Subsidies	Provision of financial assistance and guarantees.	Tourism				
Tax Obligations	None.					
Access to Financing	None.					
Government Procurement	Government employees required to use national airline.	Air transportation				
Investments by Established Companies	Foreign-owned companies participation in Turkish banks may not exceed 49 per cent.	Banking				
Investments by Established Companies	A foreign-owned bank established in Turkey is restricted in the maximum number of branches it can have (presently five) nationwide and in each city (presently one except for Istanbul).	Banking				
Investments by Established Companies	Foreign-controlled enterprises are prohibited from engaging in various sectors of business activity.	Communications, alcoholic beverages (except beer and wine), tobacco, war materials, railways, certain domestic transportation.				
Investments by Established Companies	Non-national airlines not permitted to establish their own ground handling facilities.	Air transportation				
Investments by Established Companies	Non-national airlines are not permitted to carry passengers from one national point to another.	Air transportation				

129

TURKEY: TRANSPARENCY

Category	Measure	Sector	Authority/ Administration	Automatic/ Discretionary	Motivation/ Results	Other Information
Investments by Established Companies	Foreign-controlled enterprises may not engage in public services.			Automatic		

Category	Measure	Sector	Authority/ Administration	Automatic/ Discretionary	Motivation/ Results	Other Information
Official Aids and Subsidies	None.					
Tax Obligations	None.					
Access to Financing	None.					
Government Procurement	Appointment of consultants under the Overseas Aid Programme To be considered eligible for engagement by the Ministry of Overseas Development under the Overseas Aid Programme, consultants must satisfy the following criteria: 1) The firm must carry on business in the United Kingdom, or be a projection in the developing country concerned of such a firm. Carrying on business in the United Kingdom means having a headquarters organisation and associated facilities in the United Kingdom, and not merely a registered office or accommodation address; 2) The firm must be willing to accept in sterling in London all payments due under contractual arrangements between the firm and the Ministry of Overseas Development; 3) If the firm is a partnership, the majority of the partners must be United Kingdom citizens; 4) The staff, who will perform the services to be rendered under the contractual arrangements with the Ministry of Overseas Development, must be United Kingdom citizens; 5) If the firm is organised as a company, United Kingdom citizens must have unrestricted control of the company.	Overseas Development Aid consultancy engaged in all sectors	The measure is a discretionary one and no specific regulations refer and it is administered by the Overseas Development Administration (ODA).			In the 1981/82 financial year the ODA let over 100 new contracts, these together with contract extensions let during that period, amounted to some £15m in value.

Category	Measure	Sector	Authority/ Administration	Automatic/ Discretionary	Motivation/ Results	Other Information
Investments by Established Companies	Registration of Aircraft An aircraft may not be registered in the United Kingdom unless it is owned by British subjects, citizens of the Republic of Ireland, British protected persons or bodies incorporated in some part of the Commonwealth and having their principal place of business in any part of the Commonwealth.	Civil Aviation	The legal basis is the Air Navigation Order 1980 which superseded the Air Navigation Order 1976 and the administering authority is the Civil Aviation Authority	Automatic	The right to register aircraft in the United Kingdom is restricted so as to ensure jurisdiction over the owners	
Investments by Established Companies	Air transport licences Air transport licences may not be granted by the Civil Aviation Authority to applicants if they are not United Kingdom nationals or bodies incorporated in the United Kingdom (or certain overseas territories) and controlled by United Kingdom nationals unless the Secretary of State consents to the grant of the licence. Thus non national airlines are generally not permitted to carry passengers from one national point to another.	Civil aviation	The legal basis for the measure is Section 65(3) and Section 66(3) of the Civil Aviation Act 1982	The restriction applies automatically although the waiver of it is at the discretion of the Secretary of State for Trade.	The restriction is a corollary of international civil aviation relations established under the Chicago Convention on International Civil Aviation 1944. States negotiate bilaterally for the right of their airlines to operate scheduled services on international routes. Most States have adopted similar measures.	
Investments by Established Companies	For lead-managing sterling issues in the UK domestic capital market, a principle of reciprocity was adopted whereby foreign-owned institutions which are UK-based and have the capacity in the UK to act as an issuing house are eligible to lead-manage sterling issues only if in the view of the Bank of England there are reciprocal opportunities in the foreign domestic capital market (of the institution concerned) for equivalent UK-owned institutions.	Investment banking	Bank of England	Discretionary	Reciprocity	

Category	Measure	Sector	Authority/ Administration	Automatic/ Discretionary	Motivation/ Results	Other Information
Official Aids and Subsidies	**Films** Under the Film Levy Finance Act 1981 there is a film levy collected on the prices of admissions to cinemas. The proceeds of the levy are distributed to the makers of eligible British films and to assist with training in film making. The following classes of films are normally eligible for levy payments: 1) Any British quota films, the maker of which was, throughout the time the film was being made, a person ordinarily resident in, or a company registered in, and the central management and control of whose business was exercised in any country that is a member state of the EEC; 2) Any other British film (e.g. 70 mm films) made by a maker fulfilling the requirements described in 1) above, the labour costs of which are not less than £50 per minute of playing time; 3) Any co-production film made in accordance with an international agreement to which the United Kingdom is a party. Such agreements have been concluded between the United Kingdom and Canada, France, the Federal Republic of Germany, Italy and Norway.	Cinema films	The legal powers for the measure are conferred under the Film Levy Finance Act 1981, The Films (Distribution of Levy) Regulations 1982 and The Cinematograph Films (Collection of Levy) Regulations 1968 as amended. The measure is administered by the British Film Funds Agency and the Department of Trade.	Automatic	The preservation of the infrastructure of the UK film industry	Levy distributions funded solely by industry contributions collected at the box office currently total about £4m per annum. According to the U.K. authorities, the measure ends in September 1985 and in the period until then, the Government will consider legislation to replace it.
Investments by Established Companies	Under the Industry Act 1975 a proposed transfer of control of an important United Kingdom manufacturing undertaking to a non-resident may be prohibited where the transfer is considered contrary to the interest of the United Kingdom or a substantial part of it. If it is considered that the national interest cannot appropriately be protected in any other way, property in such a proposed or completed transfer may be compulsorily acquired (vested) against compensation;	This measure applies to important undertakings which are wholly or mainly engaged in the manufacturing sector.	The legal basis is Part II of the Industry Act 1975. The powers are conferred by Act of Parliament and exercisable by Statutory Instrument. The Secretary of State by order made by Statutory Instrument which is	The measure is discretionary and and the Secretary of State would exercise it only if it was considered there was no satisfactory means of protecting the national interest.	The powers are intended to safeguard the national interests of the UK.	

UNITED KINGDOM: TRANSPARENCY

Category	Measure	Sector	Authority/Administration	Automatic/Discretionary	Motivation/Results	Other Information
	however, in the case of completed transfers, vesting may only apply to those that have occurred on or after 1 February 1975 and where the transfer came to the Government's notice within the preceding three months.		subject to the approval of both Houses of Parliament.			
Investments by Established Companies	British Aerospace PLC. The Articles of Association of British Aerospace restrict the number of foreign held shares at any one time to 15 per cent of the ordinary voting equity. The Articles also provide that the directors of the company must be British citizens or British Dependant Territories Citizens or British overseas citizens within the meaning of the British Nationalities Act 1981.	Aerospace	The legal basis for the measure are the Articles of Association of British Aerospace PLC, dated 2 January 1981, and as modified on 18 May 1982	Automatic	Her Majesty's Government considers this measure necessary to protect the UK's essential security interests. The current foreign shareholding in the company is around 5 per cent.	
Investments by Established Companies	Broadcasting. An individual may not have a controlling interest in programme companies providing programmes for transmission by the IBA unless he is either i) a national of an EEC Member State who is ordinarily resident within the European Community or ii) he is ordinarily resident in the United Kingdom, the Channel Islands or the Isle of Man (regardless of his nationality). A corporate body controlled by a disqualified person is itself disqualified.	Broadcasting	The legal basis for the restriction is the Broadcasting Act 1981, which consolidated the Independent Broadcasting Authority Act 1973 and the Broadcasting Act 1980. The measure is administered by the Head Office.	Automatic	The measure is required to preserve the national character of programme companies which exist to provide public service broadcasting for a British audience. (Until 1981 the disqualification applied to individuals normally resident and organisations incorporated outside the UK. The disqualification was changed by the Broadcasting Act 1980 to conform to UK obligations under The Treaty of Rome).	

UNITED KINGDOM: TRANSPARENCY

Category	Measure	Sector	Authority/ Administration	Automatic/ Discretionary	Motivation/ Results	Other Information
Investments by Established Companies	Importation of certain goods (sensitive stores and equipment of the armed forces) is reserved to the national flag.	Maritime trans- portation			National security	
Investments by Established Companies	A ship cannot be deemed a "British" ship unless it is owned wholly by British subjects or bodies incorpo- rated under and subject to the laws of the UK or a Commonwealth country.	Shipping	The Merchant Shipping Act 1894 is the legal basis and the adminis- tering authority is the Department of Trade.		The right to fly the British flag must be restric- ted to nationals and companies in- corporated in the UK in order to have full juris- diction over them.	

Category	Measure	Sector	Authority/ Administration	Automatic/ Discretionary	Motivation/ Results	Other Information
Official Aids and Subsidies	Foreign enterprises cannot obtain special government emergency loans for agricultural purposes after a natural disaster or government loans to individual farmers or ranchers to purchase and operate family farms.	Agriculture	Consolidated Farm and Rural Development Act, as amended/ Farmers Home Administration	Automatic	Assure effective credit services to U.S. farmers and establish threshold for participation in programme.	
Official Aids and Subsidies	Foreign-controlled enterprises may not purchase Overseas Private Investment Corporation (OPIC) insurance or guarantees.	All	Foreign Assistance Act of 1961, as amended/ Overseas Private Investment Corporation	Automatic	Assure access for US-controlled enterprises to limited government insurance and guarantees	OPIC loans and guarantees in fiscal 1982 totalled $210 million in FY 1982.
Tax Obligations	None.					
Access to Financing	None.					
Government Procurement	To be eligible for consideration by the U.S. Agency for International Development (AID) as a contractor, a company that is less than 50 per cent owned by U.S. citizens must be established in the U.S. for more than three years, have performed within the U.S. similar services under contract for services and derived revenue there from during each of the three years, employ U.S. citizens in more than half its permanent full time positions in the U.S., and have the existing capacity in the U.S. to perform the contract.	All	Agency for International Development (U.S. Agency) handbook.	Automatic	To ensure that contractors are well established in the U.S. and have the required capacity for the services offered.	Aid consultative services totalled $210 million in FY 1982.
Investments by Established Companies	Foreign-controlled enterprises operating in the U.S. may not acquire rights and of way for oil pipelines, or leases or interests therein for mining coal, oil or certain other minerals, on federal lands other than the outer continental shelf, if the alien's home country does not grant reciprocal investment privileges to U.S. citizens that are similar or like those accorded aliens.	Oil exploration and mining	Mineral Lands Leasing Act of 1920/Department of Interior	Discretionary	Reduce foreign restrictions on U.S. companies	According to the U.S. authorities only one country, not a Member of OECD, has been determined to be non-reciprocal.

136

Category	Measure	Sector	Authority/ Administration	Automatic/ Discretionary	Motivation/ Results	Other Information
Investments by Established Companies	Foreign-flag vessels may not fish in the 200 nautical mile U.S. exclusive economic zone except under the terms of a Governing International Fisheries Agreement (GIFA), or other agreement consistent with U.S. law, negotiated between the U.S. and the foreign government concerned. (As noted elsewhere, there are restrictions on ownership of U.S. flag vessels by foreign-controlled enterprises).	Fishing	Magnuson Fishery Conservation and Management Act/ National Marine Fisheries Service	Discretionary	Assist in the development of the U.S. fishing industry, fishery conservation	In 1983, the U.S. had GIFAs with 12 countries and the EC, and 1.5 million tons of fisheries resources were allocated for foreign-flag vessels.
Investments by Established Companies	Non U.S. insurers are subject to reciprocity provisions in 35 states.	Insurance (States)	State Law	Automatic and Discretionary	Reciprocity	According to the U.S. authorities, foreign insurers are accorded National Treatment in the larger States where most underwriting takes place.
Investments by Established Companies	One state forbids alien railroads from owning directly or indirectly the stock of a railroad company incorporated in that state.	Railroads (State)	State Law	Automatic	Protect local interests	Duration: indefinite
Investments by Established Companies	Four states place restrictions on alien access to mineral rights. One state has a reciprocity test.	Mining (States)	State Law	Discretionary	Limit access to U.S. citizens; reciprocity	Duration: indefinite
Investments by Established	Thirty states forbid foreign-controlled enterprises from freely owning land and impose limitations on ownership and/or use of land.	All/real estate (States)	State Law	Varies	Monitoring, limiting or prohibiting foreign ownership	Duration: indefinite

Category	Measure	Sector	Authority/ Administration	Automatic/ Discretionary	Motivation/ Results	Other Information
Official Aids and Subsidies	Foreign-controlled enterprises may not:					
	1. Obtain loan guarantees or tax deferment benefits for the financing or refinancing of the cost of purchasing, constructing or operating commercial vessels or gear, or obtain war risk insurance;	Maritime transportation		Automatic	National security, maintain strong merchant marine	Duration: indefinite
	2. Sell obsolete vessels to the Secretary of Transportation in exchange for credit towards new vessels;	Maritime transportation	Merchant Marine Act, 1936, as amended/Department of Transportation	Automatic	National security, maintain strong merchant marine	Duration: indefinite
	3. Hold a preferred ship mortgage, however foreign-controlled corporations may have a preferred ship mortgage as long as a U.S. citizen trustee holds mortgage for their benefit;	Maritime transportation	Ship Mortgage Act, 1920, as amended/ Department of Transportation	Automatic	National security, maintain strong merchant marine	Duration: indefinite
	4. Purchase vessels converted by the government for commercial use or surplus war-built vessels at a special statutory sales price;	Maritime transportation	Merchant Ship Sales Act of 1946, as amended/Dept. of Transportation	Automatic	National security, maintain strong merchant marine	Duration: indefinite
	5. Obtain construction-differential or operating-differential subsidies for vessel construction or operation.	Maritime transportation	Merchant Marine Act, 1936, as amended/Dept. of Transportation	Automatic	National security, maintain strong merchant marine	Duration: indefinite
Government Procurement	Foreign-controlled enterprises operating in the United States may not be granted a contract or subcontract involving classified information, except under special arrangements to be determined on a case-by-case basis.	Defence	U.S. Dept. of Defense Regulation 5200.22-R, Section II; Executive Orders 10865, 12064/ Department of Defense	Discretionary	National security	Duration: indefinite. Total defense procurement $64 billion in FY 1982
Government Procurement	Foreign-controlled carriers cannot compete for Federal Government contracts for international air carriage of persons or property, except in limited instances between two foreign points.	Air transportation	Federal Aviation Act of 1958/ Comptroller General of the U.S.	Automatic	National security, ensure strong domestic aviation capability	Duration: indefinite

UNITED STATES: TRANSPARENCY

Category	Measure	Sector	Authority/Administration	Automatic/Discretionary	Motivation/Results	Other Information
Government Procurement	50 per cent of goods procured or financed by U.S. Government must be shipped on privately owned U.S. flag vessels.	Maritime Transportation	Merchant Marine Act, 1936, as amended/Dept. of Transportation	Automatic	National security, maintain strong merchant marine	Duration: indefinite
Investments by Established Companies	Foreign-controlled enterprises may not acquire, mortgage or charter vessels owned by a U.S. citizen, documented under U.S. law or last documented under U.S. law, without the approval of the Secretary of Transportation. (In time of war or national emergency this provision extends to shipyard facilities and controlling interests in corporations owning such facilities or U.S. flag vessels).	Maritime transportation	Shipping Act, 1916, as amended/ Department of Transportation	Automatic	National security, ensure strong merchant marine	Duration: indefinite
Investments by Established Companies	Foreign-controlled enterprises may not own vessels which transport merchandise or passengers between U.S. ports, or which tow vessels carrying such merchandise or passengers between U.S. ports. (There are exceptions to this general rule, one of which permits a foreign-controlled U.S. manufacturing or mining company to engage in shipping activities in the U.S. coastwise trade which are related to its principal business, and transportation of cargo cannot be for hire).	Maritime transportation	Merchant Marine Act of 1920, as amended/Dept. of Transportation	Automatic	National security, ensure strong merchant marine	Duration: indefinite
Investments by Established Companies	Foreign-controlled enterprises may not engage in dredging, salvage, or certain fishing operations involving the coastwise trade.	Maritime transportation and other activities	Title 46 United States Code, Sections 251,292, 316,319; Merchant Marine Act, 1920, Fishery Conservation and Management Act/Dept. of Transportation	Automatic	National security, ensure strong merchant marine	Duration: indefinite
Investments by Established Companies	Foreign-controlled enterprises may not, except as approved by the Civil Aeronautics Board, acquire control of a U.S. air carrier if the foreign enterprise is substantially engaged	Air transportation	Federal Aviation Act of 1958, as amended/Civil Aeronautics Board	Discretionary	National security	Duration: indefinite.

Category	Measure	Sector	Authority/Administration	Automatic/Discretionary	Motivation/Results	Other Information
	in the business of aeronautics, (including a foreign air carrier), or acquire control of any U.S. company substantially engaged in the business of aeronautics if the foreign enterprise is a foreign air carrier or a person controlling such a carrier.					
Investments by Established Companies	Only an entity which is a U.S. citizen can be a U.S. air carrier and carry persons, property or mail as a common carrier for compensation or hire between points within the U.S. A corporation is a U.S. citizen only if 75 per cent or more of its voting interest is owned and controlled by U.S. citizens and the president and two-thirds or more of its management and board of directors are U.S. citizens.	Air transportation	Federal Aviation Act of 1958, as amended/Civil Aeronautics Board	Automatic	National security	Duration: indefinite
Investments by Established Companies	Foreign-controlled enterprises may not engage in operations involving the utilisation or production of atomic energy.	Nuclear Energy	Atomic Energy Act of 1954/Nuclear Regulatory Commission	Automatic	National security	Duration: indefinite
Investments by Established Companies	Foreign-controlled enterprises may not engage in radio or television broadcasting, unless the Federal Communication finds the grant of a licence to be in the public interest.	Broadcasting	Communications Act of 1934, as amended/Federal Communications Commission (FCC)	Discretionary	National security	Duration: indefinite. The F.C.C. has granted licences for such activities anciallary to other business of a foreign-controlled enterprise.
Investments by Established Companies	U.S. law does not prohibit the granting of cable landing licences to foreign-owned or controlled companies, but it is U.S. policy to grant licences only to U.S. applicants who are are in partnership with foreign entities.	Communications	Federal Policy	Discretionary; the nature of such operation generally involves enterprises of two nations which, jointly,	National security	Duration: indefinite. No applications have been made by foreign enterprises not applying jointly.

Category	Measure	Sector	Authority/ Administration	Automatic/ Discretionary	Motivation/ Results	Other Information
				apply for cable landing licences in their respective nations.		
Investments by Established Companies	Foreign-controlled enterprises may not hold in aggregate more than 20 per cent of the stock of the Communications Satellite Corporation.	Communications	Communications Satellite Act of 1962/Federal Communications Commission	Automatic	National security	Duration: indefinite
Investments by Established Companies	In order for a corporation, partnership, association or other entity organised or existing under the laws of the U.S. or of any state to obtain a licence to own, construct or operate an ocean thermal energy conversion facility located in the territorial sea of the U.S., documented under the laws of the U.S. or connected to the U.S. by pipeline or cable, the president or other executive officer and the chairman of the board of directors must be U.S. citizens and the board of directors must have no more foreign citizens serving as directors than a minority of the number of directors necessary to constitute a quorum.	Thermal energy	Ocean Thermal Energy Conversion Act of 1980/National Oceanic and Atmospheric Administration	Automatic	National security	Duration: indefinite
Investments by Established Companies	A majority of the directors of a national bank that is an affiliate or subsidiary of a foreign bank must be U.S. citizens.	Banking	International Banking Act of 1978	Automatic	Banking soundness (i.e. public order)	Duration: indefinite
Investments by Established Companies	A majority of states require that foreign and domestic insurance companies which are not resident in the state concerned obtain a licence to open a branch. Licensing requirements may differ from those of residents of the state on the following points: ownership limitations, deposit requirements, licence renewals, investment and capital requirements.	Insurance	State Law	Automatic and discretionary depending on the measure	Public order, protect consumer interest	According to the U.S. authorities, foreign interests are accorded National Treatment in all of the larger states in which most underwriting takes place.

UNITED STATES: TRANSPARENCY

Category	Measure	Sector	Authority/ Administration	Automatic/ Discretionary	Motivation/ Results	Other Information
Investments by Established Companies	To obtain a licence to operate a customs brokerage two officers or partners of a firm must be licensed customs brokers and only U.S. citizens may obtain such licences.	Customs brokerage	Tariff Act of 1930, as amended/ Department of Treasury	Automatic	Public order	Duration: indefinite
Investments by Established Companies	To engage in certain activities, a foreign-controlled enterprise operating in the United States must meet certain requirements relating to the form of its business organisation. For example, a foreign-controlled enterprise must incorporate under the laws of one of the States of the United States in order to obtain licences to construct dams, reservoirs, power houses and transmission lines.	All	Federal and State Law	Automatic	Public order	According to the U.S. authorities, likely no significant impact since incorporation under the laws of one of the States does not usually entail significant burdens.
Investments by Established Companies	For state licensed branches, or in some cases agencies, four States of the U.S. apply reciprocity considerations.	Banking (States)	State banking agencies	Automatic		According to the U.S. authorities, with the alternative of a federally licensed branch or agency, this measure is of little practical importance.
Corporate Organisation	Some States have citizenship requirements for bank incorporators or directors.	Banking (States)	State Law	Automatic	Public order (banking soundness, reciprocity)	Duration: indefinite

Annex II

THE OECD DECLARATION ON INTERNATIONAL INVESTMENT AND MULTINATIONAL ENTERPRISES, AND THE SECOND REVISED DECISIONS OF THE COUNCIL ON THE GUIDELINES FOR MULTINATIONAL ENTERPRISES AND ON INTERNATIONAL INVESTMENT INCENTIVES AND DISINCENTIVES

THE OECD DECLARATION ON INTERNATIONAL INVESTMENT AND MULTINATIONAL ENTERPRISES

THE GOVERNMENTS OF OECD MEMBER COUNTRIES

CONSIDERING

- That international investment has assumed increased importance in the world economy and has considerably contributed to the development of their countries;

- That multinational enterprises play an important role in this investment process;

- That co-operation by Member countries can improve the foreign investment climate, encourage the positive contribution which multinational enterprises can make to economic and social progress, and minimise and resolve difficulties which may arise from their various operations;

- That, while continuing endeavours within the OECD may lead to further international arrangements and agreements in this field, it seems appropriate at this stage to intensify their co-operation and consultation on issues relating to international investment and multinational enterprises through interrelated instruments of each of which deals with a different aspect of the matter and together constitute a framework within which the OECD will consider these issues:

DECLARE:

Guidelines for Multinational Enterprises	I.	That they jointly recommend to multinational enterprises operating in their territories the observance of the Guidelines as set forth in the Annex hereto having regard to the considerations and understandings which introduce the Guidelines and are an integral part of them;
National Treatment	II. 1.	That Member countries should, consistent with their needs to maintain public order, to protect their essential security interests and to fulfil commitments relating to peace and security, accord to enterprises operating in their territories and owned or controlled directly or indirectly by nationals of another Member country (hereinafter referred to as "Foreign-Controlled Enterprises") treatment under their laws, regulations and administrative practices, consistent with international law and no less favourable than that accorded in like situations to domestic enterprises (hereinafter referred to as "National Treatment");

144

2. That Member countries will consider applying "National Treatment" in respect of countries other than Member countries;

3. That Member countries will endeavour to ensure that their territorial subdivisions apply "National Treatment";

4. That this Declaration does not deal with the right of Member countries to regulate the entry of foreign investment or the conditions of establishment of foreign enterprises.

International Investment Incentives and Disincentives

III. 1. That they recognise the need to strengthen their co-operation in the field of international direct investment;

2. That they recognise the need to give due weight to the interests of Member countries affected by specific laws, regulations and administrative practices in this field (hereinafter called "measures") providing official incentives and disincentives to international direct investment;

3. That Member countries will endeavour to make such measures as transparent as possible, so that their importance and purpose can be ascertained and that information on them can be readily available;

Consultation Procedures

IV. That they are prepared to consult one another on the above matters in conformity with the Decisions of the Council relating to Inter-Governmental Consultation Procedures on the Guidelines for Multinational Enterprises, on National Treatment and on International Investment Incentives and Disincentives.

Review

V. That they will review the above matters within three years (1) with a view to improving the effectiveness of international economic co-operation among Member countries on issues relating to international investment and multinational enterprises.

NOTES AND REFERENCES

1. A first review was undertaken in 1979. The present review took place in the OECD Council meeting at Ministerial level on 17th and 18th May 1984. It was decided to review the Declaration again at the latest in six years.

SECOND REVISED DECISION OF THE COUNCIL ON THE GUIDELINES FOR
MULTINATIONAL ENTERPRISES

THE COUNCIL,

Having regard to the Convention on the Organisation for Economic Co-operation and Development of 14th December 1960 and, in particular, to Articles 2 d), 3 and 5 a) thereof;

Having regard to the Resolution of the Council of 28th November 1979, on the Terms of Reference of the Committee on International Investment and Multinational Enterprises and, in particular, to paragraph 2 thereof [C(79)210(Final)];

Taking note of the Declaration by the Governments of OECD Member countries of 21st June 1976 in which they jointly recommend to multinational enterprises the observance of guidelines for multinational enterprises;

Having regard to the Revised Decision of the Council of 13th June 1979 on Inter-Governmental Consultation Procedures on the Guidelines for Multi-national Enterprises [C(79)143];

Recognising the desirability of setting forth procedures by which consultations may take place on matters related to these guidelines;

Recognising that, while bilateral and multilateral co-operation should be strengthened when multinational enterprises are made subject to conflicting requirements, effective co-operation on problems arising therefrom may best be pursued in most circumstances on a bilateral level, although there may be cases where the multilateral approach would be more effective;

Considering the Report on the Review of the 1976 Declaration and Decisions on International Investment and Multinational Enterprises [C(79)102(Final)] and the Report on the Second Review of the 1976 Declaration and Decisions on International Investment and Multinational Enterprises [C/MIN(84)5(Final)], including the particular endorsement of the section in the Second Review Report relating to conflicting requirements;

On the proposal of the Committee on International Investment and Multi-national Enterprises:

DECIDES:

1.   Member Governments shall set up National Contact Points for undertaking promotional activities, handling enquiries and for discussions with the parties concerned on all matters related to the Guidelines so that they can contribute to the solution of problems which may arise in this connection. The business community, employee organisations and other interested parties shall be informed of the availability of such facilities.

2.   National Contact Points in different countries shall co-operate if such need arises, on any matter related to the Guidelines relevant to their

activities. As a general procedure, discussions at the national level should be initiated before contacts with other National Contact Points are undertaken.

3.   The Committee on International Investment and Multinational Enterprises (hereinafter called "the Committee") shall periodically or at the request of a Member country hold an exchange of views on matters related to the Guidelines and the experience gained in their application. The Committee shall be responsible for clarification of the Guidelines. Clarification will be provided as required. The Committee shall periodically report to the Council on these matters.

4.   The Committee shall periodically invite the Business and Industry Advisory Committee to OECD (BIAC) and the Trade Union Advisory Committee to OECD (TUAC) to express their views on matters related to the Guidelines. In addition, exchanges of views with the advisory bodies on these matters may be held upon request by the latter. The Committee shall take account of such views in its reports to the Council.

5.   If it so wishes, an individual enterprise will be given the opportunity to express its views either orally or in writing on issues concerning the Guidelines involving its interests.

6.   The Committee shall not reach conclusions on the conduct of individual enterprises.

7.   Member countries may request that consultations be held in the Committee on any problem arising from the fact that multinational enterprises are made subject to conflicting requirements. The Member countries concerned shall be prepared to give prompt and sympathetic consideration to requests by Member countries for consultations in the Committee or through other mutually acceptable arrangements, it being understood that such consultations would be facilitated by notification at the earliest stage practicable. Governments concerned will co-operate in good faith with a view to resolving such problems, either within the Committee or through other mutually acceptable arrangements.

8.   The CIME will continue to serve as a forum for consideration of the question of conflicting requirements, including, as appropriate, the national and international legal principles involved.

9.   Member countries should be prepared to assist the Committee in its periodic reviews of experience on matters relating to conflicting requirements.

10.   The Committee shall periodically invite the Business and Industry Advisory Committee to the OECD (BIAC) and the Trade Union Advisory Committee to the OECD (TUAC) to express their views on matters relating to conflicting requirements.

11.   This Decision shall be reviewed at the latest in six years. The Committee shall make proposals for this purpose as appropriate.

12.   This Decision shall replace Decision [C(79)143].

SECOND REVISED DECISION OF THE COUNCIL ON INTERNATIONAL INVESTMENT INCENTIVES AND DISINCENTIVES

THE COUNCIL,

Having regard to the Convention on the Organisation for Economic Co-operation and Development of 14th December 1960 and, in particular, Articles 2 c), 2 d), 2 e), 3 and 5 a) thereof;

Having regard to the Resolution of the Council of 28th November 1979 on the Terms of Reference of the Committee on International Investment and Multinational Enterprises [C(79)210(Final)];

Taking note of the Declaration by the Governments of OECD Member countries of 21st June 1976 on International Investment Incentives and Disincentives;

Having regard to the Revised Decision of the Council of 13th June 1979 on International Investment Incentives and Disincentives [C(79)145];

Considering the Report on the Second Review of the 1976 Declaration and Decisions on International Investment and Multinational Enterprises [C/MIN(84)5(Final)];

On the proposal of the Committee on International Investment and Multinational Enterprises;

DECIDES:

1.   Consultations will take place in the framework of the Committee on International Investment and Multinational Enterprises at the request of a Member country which considers that its interests may be adversely affected by the impact on its flow of international direct investments of measures taken by another Member country which provide significant official incentives and disincentives to international direct investment. Having full regard to the national economic objectives of the measures and without prejudice to policies designed to redress regional imbalances, the purpose of the consultations will be to examine the possibility of reducing such effects to a minimum.

2.   Member countries shall supply, under the consultation procedures, all permissible information relating to any measures being the subject of the consultation.

3.   The Committee may periodically invite the Business and Industry Advisory Committee to OECD (BIAC) and the Trade Union Advisory Committee to OECD (TUAC) to express their views on matters relating to international investment incentives and disincentives and shall take account of these views in its periodic reports to the Council.

4.   This decision shall be reviewed at the latest in six years. The Committee on International Investment and Multinational Enterprises shall make proposals for this purpose as appropriate.

5.   This decision shall replace Decision [C(79)145].

OECD SALES AGENTS
DÉPOSITAIRES DES PUBLICATIONS DE L'OCDE

ARGENTINA – ARGENTINE
Carlos Hirsch S.R.L., Florida 165, 4° Piso (Galería Guemes)
1333 BUENOS AIRES, Tel. 33.1787.2391 y 30.7122

AUSTRALIA – AUSTRALIE
Australia and New Zealand Book Company Pty, Ltd.,
10 Aquatic Drive, Frenchs Forest, N.S.W. 2086
P.O. Box 459, BROOKVALE, N.S.W. 2100. Tel. (02) 452.44.11

AUSTRIA – AUTRICHE
OECD Publications and Information Center
4 Simrockstrasse 5300 Bonn (Germany). Tel. (0228) 21.60.45
Local Agent/Agent local :
Gerold and Co., Graben 31, WIEN 1. Tel. 52.22.35

BELGIUM – BELGIQUE
Jean De Lannoy, Service Publications OCDE
avenue du Roi 202, B-1060 BRUXELLES. Tel. 02/538.51.69

CANADA
Renouf Publishing Company Limited,
Central Distribution Centre,
61 Sparks Street (Mall),
P.O.B. 1008 - Station B,
OTTAWA, Ont. KIP 5R1.
Tel. (613)238.8985-6
Toll Free: 1-800.267.4164
Librairie Renouf Limitée
980 rue Notre-Dame,
Lachine, P.Q. H8S 2B9,
Tel. (514) 634-7088.

DENMARK – DANEMARK
Munksgaard Export and Subscription Service
35, Nørre Søgade
DK 1370 KØBENHAVN K. Tel. +45.1.12.85.70

FINLAND – FINLANDE
Akateeminen Kirjakauppa
Keskuskatu 1, 00100 HELSINKI 10. Tel. 65.11.22

FRANCE
Bureau des Publications de l'OCDE,
2 rue André-Pascal, 75775 PARIS CEDEX 16. Tel. (1) 524.81.67
Principal correspondant :
13602 AIX-EN-PROVENCE : Librairie de l'Université.
Tel. 26.18.08

GERMANY – ALLEMAGNE
OECD Publications and Information Center
4 Simrockstrasse 5300 BONN Tel. (0228) 21.60.45

GREECE – GRÈCE
Librairie Kauffmann, 28 rue du Stade,
ATHÈNES 132. Tel. 322.21.60

HONG-KONG
Government Information Services,
Publications/Sales Section, Baskerville House,
2nd Floor, 22 Ice House Street

ICELAND – ISLANDE
Snaebjörn Jónsson and Co., h.f.,
Hafnarstraeti 4 and 9, P.O.B. 1131, REYKJAVIK.
Tel. 13133/14281/11936

INDIA – INDE
Oxford Book and Stationery Co. :
NEW DELHI-1, Scindia House. Tel. 45896
CALCUTTA 700016, 17 Park Street. Tel. 240832

INDONESIA – INDONÉSIE
PDIN-LIPI, P.O. Box 3065/JKT., JAKARTA, Tel. 583467

IRELAND – IRLANDE
TDC Publishers – Library Suppliers
12 North Frederick Street, DUBLIN 1 Tel. 744835-749677

ITALY – ITALIE
Libreria Commissionaria Sansoni :
Via Lamarmora 45, 50121 FIRENZE. Tel. 579751/584468
Via Bartolini 29, 20155 MILANO. Tel. 365083
Sub-depositari :
Ugo Tassi
Via A. Farnese 28, 00192 ROMA. Tel. 310590
Editrice e Libreria Herder,
Piazza Montecitorio 120, 00186 ROMA. Tel. 6794628
Costantino Ercolano, Via Generale Orsini 46, 80132 NAPOLI. Tel. 405210
Libreria Hoepli, Via Hoepli 5, 20121 MILANO. Tel. 865446
Libreria Scientifica, Dott. Lucio de Biasio "Aeiou"
Via Meravigli 16, 20123 MILANO Tel. 807679
Libreria Zanichelli
Piazza Galvani 1/A, 40124 Bologna Tel. 237389
Libreria Lattes, Via Garibaldi 3, 10122 TORINO. Tel. 519274
La diffusione delle edizioni OCSE è inoltre assicurata dalle migliori librerie nelle
città più importanti.

JAPAN – JAPON
OECD Publications and Information Center,
Landic Akasaka Bldg., 2-3-4 Akasaka,
Minato-ku, TOKYO 107 Tel. 586.2016

KOREA – CORÉE
Pan Korea Book Corporation,
P.O. Box n° 101 Kwangwhamun, SÉOUL. Tel. 72.7369

LEBANON – LIBAN
Documenta Scientifica/Redico,
Edison Building, Bliss Street, P.O. Box 5641, BEIRUT.
Tel. 354429 – 344425

MALAYSIA – MALAISIE
University of Malaya Co-operative Bookshop Ltd.
P.O. Box 1127, Jalan Pantai Baru
KUALA LUMPUR. Tel. 577701/577072

THE NETHERLANDS – PAYS-BAS
Staatsuitgeverij, Verzendboekhandel,
Chr. Plantijnstraat 1 Postbus 20014
2500 EA S-GRAVENHAGE. Tel. nr. 070.789911
Voor bestellingen: Tel. 070.789208

NEW ZEALAND – NOUVELLE-ZÉLANDE
Publications Section,
Government Printing Office Bookshops:
AUCKLAND: Retail Bookshop: 25 Rutland Street,
Mail Orders: 85 Beach Road, Private Bag C.P.O.
HAMILTON: Retail: Ward Street,
Mail Orders, P.O. Box 857
WELLINGTON: Retail: Mulgrave Street (Head Office),
Cubacade World Trade Centre
Mail Orders: Private Bag
CHRISTCHURCH: Retail: 159 Hereford Street,
Mail Orders: Private Bag
DUNEDIN: Retail: Princes Street
Mail Order: P.O. Box 1104

NORWAY – NORVÈGE
J.G. TANUM A/S
P.O. Box 1177 Sentrum OSLO 1. Tel. (02) 80.12.60

PAKISTAN
Mirza Book Agency, 65 Shahrah Quaid-E-Azam, LAHORE 3.
Tel. 66839

PORTUGAL
Livraria Portugal, Rua do Carmo 70-74,
1117 LISBOA CODEX. Tel. 360582/3

SINGAPORE – SINGAPOUR
Information Publications Pte Ltd,
Pei-Fu Industrial Building,
24 New Industrial Road N° 02-06
SINGAPORE 1953, Tel. 2831786, 2831798

SPAIN – ESPAGNE
Mundi-Prensa Libros, S.A.
Castelló 37, Apartado 1223, MADRID-1. Tel. 275.46.55
Libreria Bosch, Ronda Universidad 11, BARCELONA 7.
Tel. 317.53.08, 317.53.58

SWEDEN – SUÈDE
AB CE Fritzes Kungl Hovbokhandel,
Box 16 356, S 103 27 STH, Regeringsgatan 12,
DS STOCKHOLM. Tel. 08/23.89.00
Subscription Agency/Abonnements:
Wennergren-Williams AB,
Box 13004, S104 25 STOCKHOLM.
Tel. 08/54.12.00

SWITZERLAND – SUISSE
OECD Publications and Information Center
4 Simrockstrasse 5300 BONN (Germany). Tel. (0228) 21.60.45
Local Agents/Agents locaux
Librairie Payot, 6 rue Grenus, 1211 GENÈVE 11. Tel. 022.31.89.50

TAIWAN – FORMOSE
Good Faith Worldwide Int'l Co., Ltd.
9th floor, No. 118, Sec. 2,
Chung Hsiao E. Road
TAIPEI. Tel. 391.7396/391.7397

THAILAND – THAILANDE
Suksit Siam Co., Ltd., 1715 Rama IV Rd,
Samyan, BANGKOK 5. Tel. 2511630

TURKEY – TURQUIE
Kültur Yayinlari Is-Türk Ltd. Sti.
Atatürk Bulvari No : 191/Kat. 21
Kavaklidere/ANKARA. Tel. 17 02 66
Dolmabahce Cad. No : 29
BESIKTAS/ISTANBUL. Tel. 60 71 88

UNITED KINGDOM – ROYAUME-UNI
H.M. Stationery Office,
P.O.B. 276, LONDON SW8 5DT.
(postal orders only)
Telephone orders: (01) 622.3316, or
49 High Holborn, LONDON WC1V 6 HB (personal callers)
Branches at: EDINBURGH, BIRMINGHAM, BRISTOL,
MANCHESTER, BELFAST.

UNITED STATES OF AMERICA – ÉTATS-UNIS
OECD Publications and Information Center, Suite 1207,
1750 Pennsylvania Ave., N.W. WASHINGTON, D.C.20006 – 4582
Tel. (202) 724.1857

VENEZUELA
Libreria del Este, Avda. F. Miranda 52, Edificio Galipan,
CARACAS 106. Tel. 32.23.01/33.26.04/31.58.38

YUGOSLAVIA – YOUGOSLAVIE
Jugoslovenska Knjiga, Knez Mihajlova 2, P.O.B. 36, BEOGRAD.
Tel. 621.992

Les commandes provenant de pays où l'OCDE n'a pas encore désigné de dépositaire peuvent être adressées à :
OCDE, Bureau des Publications, 2, rue André-Pascal, 75775 PARIS CEDEX 16.

Orders and inquiries from countries where sales agents have not yet been appointed may be sent to:
OECD, Publications Office, 2, rue André-Pascal, 75775 PARIS CEDEX 16.

68236-12-1984

OECD PUBLICATIONS, 2, rue André-Pascal, 75775 PARIS CEDEX 16 - No. 43167 1985
PRINTED IN FRANCE
(21 85 01 1) ISBN 92-64-12658-9